Race Elements
in the
White Population
of
North Carolina

The Reprint Company
Spartanburg, South Carolina

The Reprint Company
Post Office Box 5401
Spartanburg, South Carolina 29301

Reprinted: 1971
ISBN 0-87152-062-1
Library of Congress Catalog Card Number: 73-149343

Manufactured in the United States of America on long-life paper

North Carolina State Normal & Industrial College Historical Publications

NUMBER 1

RACE ELEMENTS IN THE WHITE POPULATION OF NORTH CAROLINA

BY R. D. W. CONNOR

SECRETARY OF THE NORTH CAROLINA HISTORICAL COMMISSION

Issued under the Direction of the Department of History

W. C. JACKSON, EDITOR

PUBLISHED BY THE COLLEGE
1920

EDITOR'S PREFACE

In an effort to promote historical investigation and study among its own students, and do its part in preserving and putting in usable shape the rich and valuable material relating to the history of North Carolina, the Department of History of this College announces the establishment of the North Carolina State Normal and Industrial College Historical Publications.

There are unlimited opportunities in our State's history for special monographic studies, and this will be the particular though not exclusive field of work for these Publications. Studies relating to the contributions of women to the State's history will be emphasized.

The Publications have an auspicious beginning in being able to have the first three numbers contributed by R. D. W. Connor, Secretary of the North Carolina Historical Commission, and Lecturer on North Carolina History at this College during 1912, 1913, 1914.

Number 3 of the Publications was published in 1914; number 2 appeared in 1916, and number 1, after much unavoidable delay, is now ready for the press.

THE EDITOR.

PREFATORY NOTE

These five lectures were delivered at the North Carolina State Normal and Industrial College for Women in the winter of 1912. They are printed here just as they were delivered. The purpose for which they were prepared did not admit of a full and elaborate discussion of the subject; designed to stimulate interest which might lead to further study, the treatment is purposely "sketchy" and general, rather than detailed. As an aid to any who may care to go further into the subject, a brief, but by no means complete bibliography is added composed of books easily accessible to any person into whose hands these lectures may chance to fall.

R. D. W. Connor.

Raleigh, N. C.
December 10, 1919.

TABLE OF CONTENTS

I

Race Elements in the White Population of North Carolina

INTRODUCTORY

The history of North Carolina during the past decade has been characterized by a remarkable development along two parallel lines, one leading to a widespread material prosperity, the other to a popular intellectual renaissance. Neither would have been possible without the other. One manifests itself in the hum of mills, the shriek of whistles, the rush and roar of trains, personifying the power and energy of an awakening people. The other, no less a personification of power, is nevertheless a silent movement, the energy of which is generated in the quiet of the school room and the closet of the student. Both movements are the results of forces that for two and a half centuries have been shaping our history and controlling our destiny, and because we are just beginning to recognize this fact, we are turning more and more to the past to seek therein an explanation of the present and a forecast of the future.

One of the most striking features of this intellectual awakening is the recent rapid development of our historical consciousness. Out of it have sprung such activities as the creation of numerous historical and patriotic societies, the preservation of battlefields and historic houses, the marking of historic sites, the celebration of historical anniversaries, and the numerous other methods by which mankind has always preserved the history of the race. In the past decade alone we have erected in North Carolina more monuments and written more books than in all the previous two hundred and fifty years of our history.

The development of the inward spirit, of which these activities are but the outward manifestations, means much in the life of our people. "The spirit of a people," says Captain Mason, "is the history of a people impersonated in the life of a people. If there is no history of a people there is no spirit of a people".[1] Without such a spirit the people perish. It seems to me, therefore, that nothing can be more important to a democratic people than the cultivation of such a spirit. Great and rapid material development may prove anything but an unmixed blessing if it be not accompanied by a corresponding development of the mental and moral resources of the State, and there is no better way to develop such resources and to strengthen this side of our life than by the study of history. Such study broadens the intelligence, strengthens the character, and confirms the patriotism of the people, and when the day of trial and stress comes, as such days do come to all people, these qualities become the chief assets of a democratic State.

"A democracy," said Dr. C. Alphonso Smith, "can not afford to be ungrateful. Built as it is on loyal service and patriotic sacrifice, the day of its forgetting will be the day of its undermining. Other nations trace their origin back through a long series of suc-

---

1. The Value of Historical Memorials in a Democratic State (*Publications of the North Carolina Historical Commission, Bulletin No. 7, p. 90*).

cessful and unsuccessful wars. We find our national genesis in a single war; and the measure of our greatness and stability will be the measure of our gratitude to the men who made Yorktown possible. . . . . National unity and stability must be built upon a foundation of common sympathies, sacrifices and triumphs. Every battlefield of the Revolution, where American valor was tested and not found wanting, will yet become a link in the golden chain of national brotherhood. The men who fought here and the men who have since wrought here are nation builders. Slowly but surely the truth of history is widening its domain, and a heroic past is returning to make a heroic and united present."[2]

The State of North Carolina has erected this college and her other institutions of learning for the purpose of training her young men and young women in the duties of citizenship in a democracy. Every function which we are called upon to perform as citizens comes to us out of the past moulded into shape by its influence and charged with its spirit. This influence we must understand, this spirit we must appreciate if we are to perform the duties and meet the responsibilities of citizenship intelligently and effectively. It follows, therefore, that a knowledge of the history of the people among whom we are to live and work is a very necessary part of our equipment for citizenship.

"Know thyself" is a wise injunction that applies to a commonwealth and its people with no less force than to an individual. What are the chief geographical features of the State in which we are to work? Whence

---

2. The Significance of History in a Democracy (*Publications of the North Carolina Historical Commission, Bulletin No. 6.*)

came its people? What are their characteristics? Their needs? Their capabilities? Wherein are they strong? Wherein weak? In what virtues do they need to be strengthened? In what vices do they need to be curbed? How have they borne themselves in the great crises of the Republic's history? Bravely? Openly? Effectively? Or have they been cowardly in battle? Secretive in council? Sloven in work? What have they wrought that is worthy the admiration of mankind? Have they contributed aught to the science of human government? To the well-being of society? To the industrial development of the world? What are their ideals? Their aspirations? Their hopes and desires? Have they made any contribution to literature? To art? To knowledge? Finally, and above all, what spirit has animated them as they have gone about their tasks, faced their responsibilities, and done their work?

In the course of these lectures which your President has asked me to deliver here, I cannot hope to do more than suggest answers to these inquiries. But if they shall help to stimulate in any of you a greater interest in the history of North Carolina and her people, to develop in your hearts and minds a larger and more intelligent State pride, and to confirm in you the convictions already implanted in you by the influence and teaching of this college that North Carolina is worthy of your very best thoughts and most earnest endeavors,— if I can contribute even in but a small degree to these ends, I shall have accomplished all that I hope to do.

It is a common statement frequently heard in public addresses and seen in public print that the population of North Carolina is composed of almost pure English stock and contains but a negligible percentage of for-

eign elements. If by foreign elements is meant persons
born in other countries than the United States, the
percentage contained in the population of North Carolina is indeed negligible; but if the phrase means other
stock than English—and this indeed is the sense in
which it is generally used in this connection—the statement is not correct. Speaking now with reference only
to the white race, the population of North Carolina of
today is a composite population made up of a mixture
of four racial elements,—first, the commercially-
minded, law-abiding, self-reliant Anglo-Saxon; second,
the Celtic Scotch-Highlander, picturesque, proud and
sensitive; third, the democratic, liberty-loving, religi-
ously-minded Scotch-Irishman; and finally, the German, shrewd, economical, conservative, a lover of
learning and of religion. By these peoples, and their
descendants, the history of North Carolina has been
made and her destiny has been shaped; and the typical
North Carolinian of the twentieth century is neither
Saxon, nor Celt, nor Teuton, but is the off-spring of
the three.

It is my purpose, in these lectures to discuss the
origin and characteristics of these races in North Carolina during the colonial period and to suggest very
briefly the contributions of each to the history of the
State.

The history of North Carolina begins with the coming of the English. Driven on by the Anglo-Saxon's
keen, insatiable hunger for land, Englishmen about the
middle of the seventeenth century crossed the Virginia
boundary line, sought out the rich bottom lands along
the shores of Albemarle Sound, and there laid the
foundations of the State. In all parts of the world
wherever the Englishman has gone in any considerable

numbers, whether in India, in South Africa, in Australia, or in America, he has carried with him the social, industrial, political and intellectual customs of his native island. The English ideal of home life, the English industrial system, the English principles of politics and government, the English language and literature sooner or later become the dominant forces wheresoever the Englishman sets up his household gods. North Carolina has been no exception to this rule. Although the first English settlers were speedily followed by the Scotch and the Germans in large numbers, who spread out over many of the choicest portions of the country, yet the customs, the government, and the language of North Carolina from the first have been those of the English settlers on the Albemarle. A study of this English settler reveals to us a prosy, commonplace individual, possessed of an immeasurable amount of hard, commonsense, whose chapter in our history has been more instructive than romantic. In him we find all the qualities essential for the conquest of the wilderness and the founding of a commonwealth. He had courage, foresight, determination, and he possessed, too, the instincts of the home-maker and an intense devotion to liberty, law, and justice according to English conceptions and English standards. To him we owe it that these standards were firmly planted in the soil of North Carolina. His struggles to preserve in the wild woods of Carolina the great principles of liberty which his forefathers had wrung from the mailed hands of tyrant kings in the wild woods of Britain, no doubt frequently led him into excesses and violences. But what of it! Shall we not pardon something to the spirit of liberty? Truly does an eloquent Carolinian exclaim: "If, in their remoteness and isola-

tion, our ancestors ever strayed into lawlessness, it
was the light struck from violated law by the mailed
hand of oppression that led them astray. . . . .
Their conduct was simply a pure and priceless demon-
stration of the political genius and self-governing passion of the Anglo-Saxon race."[3] During the early
years of our history these English settlers took up arms
and went forth to battle more than once in defense of
their ideals of constitutional liberty and achieving success at last, they wrote them imperishably into the
Constitution of 1776 whence they have been handed
down to us as our most precious legacy.

But if we find the English settler on the Albemarle
prosaic and unromantic, we shall find his Scotch neigh-
bor on the upper Cape Fear picturesque and interesting enough. The genius of Sir Walter Scott has
thrown a halo of romance about the Scotch-Highlander
as he appears on his native heath which he does not
lose even amid the forests of America. The Highlanders were a strong and active race, large in stature, well
developed in body, robust in health. Their wild life
among their native highlands imposed upon them occupations that developed strength and courage and
activity both of mind and body. Following the chase
over pathless mountains, waging constant warfare
among themselves and with their neighbors of the lowlands, had trained them to a keenness of sight and swift-
ness of limbs that rivalled those characteristics in the
American Indian. Their wild romantic life developed
in them "firmness of decision, fertility in resources,
ardor in friendship, love of country, and generous en-

3. Alderman, E. A.: William Hooper, "The Prophet of
American Independence," pp. 13-15.

thusiasm." Brought up to the use of arms in the midst of perpetual violence, accustomed to occupations requiring great physical endurance and courage, the Highlanders were taught to admire to excess physical strength and prowess, to bear without complaint the severest hardships, and to despise the comforts and luxuries of civilized society as fit only for effeminate cowards.

It was during the decade from 1730 to 1740 that the Highlanders began to come to North Carolina. Oppressed by both political and economic tyranny in their native land, many thousands of them sought relief by turning their faces to the setting sun. Shipload after shipload reached the shores of the New World, and most of them found their way to the Cape Fear in North Carolina. Bringing with them their picturesque costumes and their peculiar customs which in Europe had made them a race apart, they attempted to reproduce on the Cape Fear the life which they had lived on the Clyde. In their new homes comfort and plenty, if not luxury and wealth, awaited them, and they soon attained in North Carolina to a degree of prosperity that in their Highland homes would have been counted wealth. And yet they did not soon forget their native land. In the forests of the New World, as far as possible, they kept up their native customs and spoke the language of their fathers. They still wore their picturesque costumes, and when they met the English at Moore's Creek Bridge in 1776 many of them were armed with the weapons their fathers had worn to battle at Culloden.

The Revolution wrought great changes in their lives. A new nation was born and the Highlanders were forced to adapt themselves to the new order. Gradually they changed their costumes to suit their new conditions, their language to suit their new associates, and their customs to suit their new country. As the older leaders died out, others who had not known the beauties and the glories of the Highlands, come to fill their places. Thus the life of the Old World passed away and that of the New World took its place. To this New World, whose history has been so enriched and colored by this splendid race, the descendants of the Highlanders have brought the same abiding love and loyalty which their fathers so faithfully gave to the old.

To the west of the Highlanders we find another element of Scotch population, which differed in many important particulars from their brethren of the upper Cape Fear and bore a closer resemblance to their English cousins of the east. These were the Scotch-Irish who began to find their way to the New World about the beginning of the second quarter of the eighteenth century. Landing for the most part at Philadelphia, they followed the course marked out by the foothills of the Alleghany Mountains, until they had dispersed themselves in small settlements throughout the Piedmont regions of Virginia and North Carolina. Piling their furniture in creaking wagons and on pack-horses, with the women and children insecurely and uncomfortably seated on top, while the men walked or rode horseback alongside, they followed the rivers and valleys until they found lands that suited them and then pitched their tents and began to build their log cabins. During a single winter more than a thousand of their wagons passed through the little village of Salisbury. Another stream of these settlers, landing at Charleston, moved up the banks of the Yadkin, the Catawba and the Broad rivers until they met the stream from Pennsylvania. Before the outbreak of the Revolution the Scotch-Irish had scattered all through the hills and valleys and along the river banks of Central North Carolina, adding to our population an element that has written many of the best chapters in our history. Sensitive about his rights, he was ever ready in the fear of God to defend them with a calm, cool, unflinching courage. "Kings and governors were kings and governors to him only so long as they obeyed the law and were faithful to the rights of the people. . . . . His liberty consisted in laws made by the consent of the people, and the due execution of those laws. He was free not from the law, but by the law." With this love of liberty, the Scotch-Irishman joined in close union a stern religious faith and an intense love of learning. The "church and the schoolhouse followed them as shadows follow the sun." Among no other element of our population have the minister and the teacher exercised so general an influence, or held so conspicuous a place in leadership. Of the Scotch-Irish, therefore, we may say that he brought with him a love of liberty as intense as that of the Englishman, but carrying with it less reverence for constitutional forms and legal precedents. Less ardent in his nature than the Highlander, he displayed in the early crisis of our history a sounder political judgment and a calmer temperament; he had a religious faith as deep but not so emotional; though not so picturesque and interesting, he has been a more conservative force in our history and has added a greater stability to our character as a people.

From Pennsylvania, following the same route as the Scotch-Irish, came a fourth element in our population who became near neighbors of the Scotch. These were industrious and thrifty Germans who settled along the waters of the Yadkin and Catawba rivers. A few of these came as adventurers to follow careers as hunters and trappers. Others came in search of cheap land. Still others came for religious reasons, cheerfully braving the dangers of the sea and the hardships of the wilderness in their search for religious freedom. Side by side with their cabins, went up their schoolhouses and churches. Like the Highlanders they brought the language and customs of the Old World to their homes in the New World. The German was the language of their church services. Their teachers taught it in their schools, and their children's textbooks were written in it. The older people clung tenaciously to it. It was the language of their cradles, of their altars, and of their firesides. Their ministers used it when they baptised them. They were married by a German service. They had heard the funeral sermons of their mothers and fathers preached in the German. All their sacred memories were connected with it. But they too had to face the same hard experience as the Scotch-Highlanders, for their descendants gradually dropped their fathers' tongue for that of their new home. The Germans were thrifty, industrious and intelligent. They practiced an unbounded hospitality, and in their homes were open-hearted, simple, conscientious and independent. Though always law-abiding, they took but little active interest in politics. But in their industrial affairs they set an example that their Scotch and English countrymen might well have imitated. All the early travelers praise them for their neat and tidy homes, their clean and well cultivated farms, their fat, sleek cattle, and their bountiful barns and pantries.

2

The center of the German settlement was the church and schoolhouse; their chief book was the Bible of Luther. They were a gentle lovable people, domestic in their habits, peaceful in their deportment, frank and open in their speech and manner, shrewd but honest in their business dealings.

Estimates of the population of North Carolina at different periods prior to the census of 1790 vary widely; there are, however, sufficient data to justify us in estimating the total population in 1760 at 130,-000. The same data lead to the conclusion that at that time the English formed a little more than a third, the Scotch about one-third, the Germans less than one-ninth, and negro-slaves about one-fourth of the total. Rejecting all other elements of European origin,—i. e., French, Swiss and Welsh—as too small to be taken into account, and also rejecting the Indians, we arrive at the following analysis of the population of North Carolina in 1760:

English 45,000
Scotch (Highlanders and Scotch-Irish) 40,000
Germans 15,000
Negroes 30,000

Total 130,000

The English and Scotch were born subjects of the British Crown; the Germans, therefore, were the only important foreign element in the white population. To place them, and those who claimed titles to property derived from them, upon an equality with the English and Scotch, the Assembly, in 1764, enacted "that all Foreign Protestants heretofore inhabiting within this Province, and dying seized of any Lands,

Tenements, or Hereditaments, shall, forever hereafter,
be deemed, taken, and esteemed to have been natural-
ized, and entitled to all the Rights, Privileges, and
Advantages of natural Born Subjects."

Such are the people who have made the history of
North Carolina and from whom the modern North
Carolinian has sprung. You cannot understand him
unless you understand his origin and the influences
that have shaped his life. He possesses the Englishman's love of home, hatred of tyranny, and respect
for constitutional forms and precedents; the Highlander's unflinching loyalty to a cause or a leader, high
sense of personal dignity and honor, and intense pas-
sions usually well under control but fierce and terrible when aroused; the Scotch-Irishman's deep spiritual
nature, stern, uncompromising religious faith, and devotion to religious liberty; and the German's simplicity
of manner, frankness of speech, and honest shrewdness
in business. It is with the hope that we may get an
insight into the character of this modern North Carolinian in whose hands lies the future of this Commonwealth that I shall present to you in my subsequent
lectures a study of each of the races from which he has
sprung.

II

The English in North Carolina

Sometime between the years 1653 and 1660 pioneers of English blood began to find their way from Virginia to the shores of Albemarle Sound where they laid the foundations of North Carolina.

A glance at the map will show why North Carolina received its first permanent settlers from Virginia. The dangerous character of the Carolina coast and the absence of good harborage made the approach too difficult and uncertain to admit of colonization directly from Europe. This became apparent from Sir Walter Raleigh's failure in his first attempt to plant a colony on Roanoke Island, and in 1587 Raleigh himself directed John White in command of the second colony to seek a site on Chesapeake Bay. His commands, through no fault of White's, were not obeyed, and the colony failed. Twenty-two years later the London Company, guided by Raleigh's experience, directed the Jamestown colony towards the Chesapeake. The first settlers, for obvious reasons, sought lands lying along navigable streams; consequently the water courses to a large extent determined the direction of the colony's growth. Many of the streams of Southeastern Virginia flow toward Currituck and Albemarle sounds in North Carolina; and the sources of the most important rivers of Eastern North Carolina are in Virginia. Furthermore the soil, the climate, the vegetation, and the animal life of the Albemarle region are of the same character as those of Southeastern Virginia. It should be remembered, too, that until 1663 this region was an organic part of Virginia. Nothing, therefore, was more natural than that the planters of Virginia searching for good bottom lands, should gradually extend their plantations southward along the shores of Albemarle Sound and the rivers that flow into it.

The Virginians early manifested a lively interest in the Albemarle region. Nansemond county, Virginia, which adjoins North Carolina, was settled as early as 1609, and during the following years many an adventurous hunter, trader, and explorer made himself familiar with the waters that pour into Albemarle and Currituck sounds. During the next thirty years the Virginia authorities sent numerous expeditions into what is now Eastern North Carolina,[1] and the sons of Governor Yeardley boasted in 1654 that the northern country of Carolina was explored by "two Virginians born."[2]

These expeditions were naturally followed by a southward movement of settlers, but just when this movement began cannot be stated with accuracy. In 1653 Roger Green, a clergyman of Nansemond county, who had become interested in the Albemarle section, obtained a grant of ten thousand acres for the first one hundred persons who should settle on Roanoke River, south of Chowan, and one hundred acres for himself "as a reward for his own first discovery and for his encouragement of the settlement."[3] Whether he followed this grant with an actual settlement is not known, but certain it is that by the year 1660 George Durant, John Battle, Thomas Relfe, Roger

1. Reports of these expeditions may be found in Colonial Records of North Carolina, Vol. I., W. L. Saunders, editor, and in Narratives of Early Carolina, 1650-1708, S. A. Salley, editor.
2. Salley, S. A.—Narratives of Early Carolina, 25-29.
3. Colonial Records of North Carolina, I., 17.

Williams, Thomas Jarvis, and others, had purchased
lands from the Indians who dwelt along the waters
of Albemarle Sound and had settled there.[4]   Many
others encouraged by their example followed these adventurous leaders, and in 1665 the surveyor of Albemarle declared that a county "fortie miles square will
not comprehend the Inhabitants there already seated."[5]
These settlers for the most part, came from Virginia;
but others came also and at the close of the first decade
of its history the Albemarle colony contained fourteen
hundred inhabitants between sixteen and sixty years
of age, and the settlements extended from Chowan
River to Currituck Sound.

It is worthy of note, as illustrative of the character
of these early settlers, that they came not as conquerors driving the natives from their hunting-grounds and
seizing their lands by force, but that in every instance
they came with peaceful purpose to purchase for valuable considerations the land which the native population willingly sold.   Indeed, so universal was this
practice that in 1662 the English government, which
wished all land titles to be derived from the Crown,
ordered that titles purchased from the Indians should
be disregarded and that no grants should be held valid
unless taken out according to the law of Virginia.   The
oldest grant for land now extant in North Carolina is
that from the Indian Chief Kilcocanen to George
Durant, dated March 1, 1661, and now on file in the
courthouse of Perquimans county.   This grant recites
the fact that, "for a valeiable consideration," and "with
the consent of my people," Kilcocanen had sold to

---

4. C. R., I., 59-67.
5. Ibid, I., 99.

George Durant "a parcel of land lying and being on
Roanoke Sound and on a river called by the name of
Perquimans."[6] Thus more than twenty years before
William Penn's celebrated treaty, George Durant pur-
chased for a valuable consideration the lands which he
might have seized by force and laid the foundations of
North Carolina in peace and goodwill rather than in
bloodshed and hatred.

From Albemarle population moved slowly southward. The stages of its progress may be marked by
the four principal river systems of Eastern Carolina—
the Roanoke, the Pamlico, the Neuse, and the Cape
Fear. No definite record of the progress of the settlements is found until they reached Pamlico River,
where in 1691 a small party of French Huguenots
from Virginia planted a colony. A few years later a
pestilence among the Indians opened the way for other
settlers, who continued to drift southward from Albemarle. By 1696 the settlement was considered of sufficient importance to be erected into a county called
Archdale, afterwards Bath, extending from the Albemarle to the Neuse, and to be allowed two representatives in the General Assembly. In 1704 a site for a
town was selected, and the next year the town was
incorporated under the name of Bath. At the close of
its first five years Bath could boast of a public library
and a dozen houses. Though at times the home of
wealth and culture, Bath never became more than a
sleepy little village, and derives its chief distinction
from the unimportant fact that it was the first town
in the province. The settlers on the Pamlico, however,
prospered and their good reports induced others to

---

6. C. R., I., 19.

join them. Two years after the founding of Bath, another body of Huguenots from Virginia, "considerable in numbers," passed the Pamlico and occupied lands on the Neuse and Trent rivers. Here in 1710 they were joined by a colony of German palatines, who had been driven from their native land on account of their religious faith.

The settlements on the Pamlico and the Neuse do not concern us here since they were not made by an English-speaking people. They were rather a small wedge of foreign population driven in between the two English settlements which during the early history of North Carolina controlled and dominated the affairs of the colony,—viz: the settlement on the Albemarle and the settlement on the Cape Fear. An attempt had been made to plant an English colony on the Cape Fear River as early as 1665, but after two years of hardship the settlement was abandoned. Thereafter the Cape Fear section fell into disrepute, and more than half a century passed before another attempt was made to plant a settlement there. Four causes contributed to this delay: first, the dangerous character of the coast; second, the hostility of the Cape Fear Indians; third, the pirates who sought refuge in large numbers behind the sand bars at the mouth of the Cape Fear River; and finally an order of the Lords Proprietors forbidding settlers to take up lands in that section.

The character of the coast, of course, could not be changed, and to this day, in spite of all that modern engineering skill can do, remains a serious obstacle to the development of a splendid section. The Cape Fear Indians "were reckoned the most barbarous of any in the colony," and stood for many years a menac-

ing barrier to those who cast longing eyes upon the
fertile lands along the Cape Fear River and its tributaries.   But finally in 1715 their power was broken
and they were overthrown.   Three years later through
the exertions of the Governor of South Carolina the
last of the pirates, after a desperate battle, was captured, carried to Charleston, and hanged at "the tail
of ae tow."

But the struggles of the Carolina settlers with the
forces of nature, the savages of the wilderness, and the
freebooters of the sea, to recover this splendid region
for civilization, were to avail nothing if they were to
yield obedience to the orders of the Lords Proprietors.
Fortunately, there were men in North Carolina who
would not consent for a few wealthy landowners beyond the sea to prevent their clearing and settling this
inviting region in the name of civilization, and about
the year 1723 the ring of their axes began to break the
long silence of the Cape Fear.   They laid off their
claims, cleared their fields, and built their cabins without regard to the formalities of law, and when the
colonial authorities saw that the people were determined to take up land without either acquiring titles
or paying rents, they decided that their own interests
would be served by giving the one and receiving the
other.

Accordingly the orders were rescinded, and good
titles thus assured, settlers were not wanting.   Governor
Burrington himself, Maurice Moore and his brother
Roger, led the way, followed by the Moseleys, the
Howes, the Porters, the Lillingtons, the Ashes, the
Harnetts, and many others whose names are closely
identified with the history of North Carolina.   On the
west bank of the Cape Fear, about fourteen miles

above its mouth, Maurice Moore laid off a town, and donated sites for a graveyard, a church, a courthouse, a markethouse, and other public buildings, and a commons "for the use of the inhabitants of the town." With an eye to royal favor he named the place Brunswick, in honor of the reigning family of Great Britain. But Burnswick, like Bath, did not flourish, and in the course of a few years after a strenuous and stormy struggle for existence, it yielded with no good grace to a younger and more vigorous rival sixteen miles farther up the river, which had been named in honor of Spencer Compton, Earl of Wilmington. The population of the Cape Fear settlement increased rapidly, and by the close of the first decade a number of fine estates were scattered up and down the banks of the Cape Fear and its tributaries. Large tracts of forest lands had been converted into beautiful meadows and cultivated plantations; comfortable, if not elegant farm houses dotted the river banks; and two towns had sprung into existence. The forest offered tribute to the lumberman and the turpentine distiller; a number of sawmills had been erected; many of the planters were engaged in the production of lumber and naval stores; and a brisk trade had been established with the other colonies and even with the mother country. When the settlement was less than ten years old, Governor Johnston declared that the inhabitants were a "sober and industrious set of people," that they had made "an amazing progress in their improvement," and that the Cape Fear had become the "place of the greatest trade in the whole province."[7]

---

7. For a more detailed account of the settlement of the Cape Fear see the author's "Cornelius Harnett: An Essay in North Carolina History," Ch. I.

As already pointed out most of the settlers on the
Albemarle and many of those on the Cape Fear came
from Virginia. But many others came also, attracted
by the cheap and fertile lands, hailing from South
Carolina, Pennsylvania, Maryland, New Jersey, New
York, and the New England colonies. From beyond
the Atlantic came hardy adventurers from England,
Scotland, and Ireland, as well as from Barbadoes,
Jamaica, and other islands of the sea. It is not without interest to note that many of those from England
hailed from localities whose names are now found
scattered all over the map of North Carolina. This
one describes himself as "late of Southwark Parish in
the County of Surry;" that one is from Dover in ye
County of Kent;" another is "from Halifax, in ye
County of York;" while still another tells us that he
was "late of Droughton near Skipton in Craven in the
County of York in Great Britain."[8] During the first
three quarters of a century, i. e., 1660-1730, the population of North Carolina, with the unimportant excep-
tions of a few French on the Pamlico and a few Germans on the Neuse, was almost entirely English. It was
these English settlers then who led the way into the
Carolina wilderness, drove back the forces of barbarism, and laid the foundations of the Commonwealth.

Historians do not agree in their delineation of the
character of these founders of our State and civilization. There are those, of whom perhaps George Davis,
the historian of the Cape Fear, was the most eminent,
who would have us believe that the settlers of the
colony "were no needy adventurers, driven by neces-

---

8. For further illustrations see Grimes, J. Bryan (editor):
   Abstracts of North Carolina Wills.

sity—no unlettered boors, ill at ease in the haunts of civilization, and seeking their proper sphere amidst the barbarism of the savage," but that 'they were gentlemen of birth and education, bred in the refinements of polished society, and bringing with them ample fortunes, gentle manners, and cultivated minds."[9]   On the other hand there are William Byrd, John Fiske, and others of their school who could see in Colonial North Carolina nothing more than "a kind of backwoods for Virginia," "an Alsatia for insolvent debtors," "mean white trash," and "outlaws," from the northern colony.   John Fiske divided the early settlers of North Carolina into two classes: first, the thriftless, improvident white servant class who could not maintain a respectable existence for themselves in Virginia; second, the "outlaws who fled [from Virginia] into North Carolina to escape the hangman."[10] Neither picture is true, for if Davis insists that the shield is all gold, none the less does Fiske insist that it is all of a baser metal.   The truth lies between.   Undoubtedly there were enough well-born educated leaders among the population to give a cultured atmosphere to the best society in the colony; and undoubtedly there were also enough escaped outlaws to keep the officers of the criminal law ever vigilant.   But both together constituted no larger percentage of the population of North Carolina than of the other colonies and in none of them were they more than a very small minority.   Between the two extremes, constituting then as now the bone and sinew of the population, were those sturdy, enterprising, law-abiding, and deeply

9. University Address, 1855.
10. Old Virginia and Her Neighbours, II, 316.

moral middle-class Englishmen who have always from Crécy and Agincourt to Yorktown and Gettysburg formed the strength and character of English-speaking nations.

The best contemporary account of the social and industrial life of the colony during the first seventy-five years of its existence is that found in Brickell's "Natural History of North Carolina," published in 1737.[11] The author was a physician and scientist of marked ability whose residence for several years in the colony gave him ample opportunity for observation. Says he: "The Europeans or Christians of North Carolina are a straight, well-limbed and active people . . . . The men who frequent the woods, and labour out of doors, or use the waters, the vicinity of the sun makes impressions on them; but as for the women who do not expose themselves to the weather, they are often very fair, and well-featured, as you shall meet with anywhere, and have very brisk and charming eyes; and as well and finely shaped as any women in the world. . . . . The children . . . are very docile and apt to learn anything as any children in Europe, and those that have the advantage to be educated write good hands and prove good accountants . . . The young men are generally of a bashful, sober behaviour, few proving prodigals, to spend what the parents with care and industry have left them, but commonly improve it . . . The girls are not only bred to the needle and spinning, but to the dairy and domestic affairs, which many of them manage with a great deal of prudence and conduct, though they are very young.

---

11. References are to Grimes' edition published by the Board of Trustees of the State Library, 1910.

. . . Both sexes are very dextrous in paddling and managing their canoes, both men, women, boys, and girls, being bred to it from infancy. . . . The men are very ingenious in several handicraft businesses, and in building their canoes and houses. . . . There are throughout this settlement as good bricks as any I ever met with in Europe. All sorts of handicrafts, such as carpenters, coopers, bricklayers, plasterers, shoemakers, tanners, tailors, weavers, and most other sorts of tradesmen, may with small beginnings, and good industry, soon thrive well in this place and provide good estates and all manner of necessaries for their families. . . . Their furniture, as with us, consists of pewter, brass, tables, chairs, which are imported here commonly from England. The better sort have tolerable quantities of plate, with other convenient, ornamental and valuable furniture."

Land and slaves were then, as they continued to be throughout the South until 1865, the chief form of wealth in North Carolina. Consequently the growth of towns was very slow and life in the colony was seen at its best on the great estates of the planters scattered along the banks of the rivers and their tributaries. Many of these planters counted from five to ten thousand acres in their estates, while not a few were lords of princely domains embracing from fifty to seventy-five thousand acres, and were masters of as many as two hundred and fifty slaves. The river courses afforded the best sites for plantations not only because of the greater fertility of the bottom lands, but also because transportation was carried on chiefly by water. At the planter's wharf sloops, schooners, and brigantines were loaded with cargoes of skins, salt pork and beef, tallow, staves, naval stores, lumber, tobacco, rice,

and other produce of the plantation to be carried away
to the West Indies and exchanged for rum, molasses,
sugar and coffee, or to Boston where the proceeds were
invested in clothing, household furniture, books and
negroes.

On an elevated site overlooking the river and generally approached through a long avenue of oaks or
cedars, was the "Manor House," or as the negroes
called it the "Big House." As a rule these mansions
were wooden buildings without any pretense to archi-
tectural beauty, though a few of the wealthier planters,
during the years preceding the Revolution, erected
brick structures after the style now known as "colonial." These colonial residences were characterized by
huge white columns, broad verandas, wide halls, large
and spacious rooms. Whether of wood or brick all
were the seats of unbounded hospitality. "The planters," says Brickell, "[are] the most hospitable people
that are to be met with," while John Lawson, who
wrote nearly thirty years earlier than Brickell, tells
us that "the planters [are] hospitable to all that come
to visit them; there being very few housekeepers but
what live very nobly and give away more provisions
to coasters and guests who come to see them than they
expend among their own families." Hospitality to
strangers and travelers was regarded as a patriotic
duty which the wealthy planters, owing to the absence
of inns and comfortable taverns, felt impelled to exercise for the honor of the province. Indeed, in their
isolated situation, a garrulous traveler or a genial
sea-captain who brought news of the outside world, was
ever an honored and a welcome guest, for whom the
housekeeper brought out her finest silver and china
ware, her best linen and her most tempting morsels,

while the planters regaled him with the choicest liquid refreshments which his cellar afforded, for as Brickell assures us, "the better sort, or those of good economy" kept "plenty of wine, rum, and other liquors at their own houses, which they generally make use of amongst their friends and acquaintances, after a most decent and discreet manner."

Every great plantation was almost a complete community in itself. Each had its own shops, mills, distillery, tannery, spinning wheels and looms, and among the slaves were to be found excellent blacksmiths, carpenters, millers, shoemakers, spinners, and weavers, and other artisans. "The clothing used by men," Brickell tells us, "are English cloaths, druggets, durois, green linen, etc. The women have their silks, calicoes, stamp-linen, calimanchoes, and all kinds of stuffs some whereof are manufactured in the Province. They make few hats, though they have the best furs in plenty, but with this article, they are commonly supplied from New England, and sometimes from Europe." In their homes the planters and their families were supplied not only with all the necessities of a pioneer community, but enjoyed many of the comforts and luxuries usually found only in a long established society.

An examination of their wills, inventories, and other documents shows among their household furniture an ample supply of those fine old mahogany tables, bedsteads, couches, chairs, and desks which excite the envy of modern housekeepers and deplete the purses of modern husbands. That the Carolina housekeeper was prepared at any time to play the hospitable hostess to the most particular guest or the most pompous colonial potentate who might chance to honor her board, is

well attested by the excellent silver, china, and glass-
ware which adorned her sideboard. The diamond
rings, earrings, necklaces, and other jewelry which the
colonial dame passed down as heirlooms to her children and grandchildren show clearly enough from
whom the twentieth century dame inherited her love of
finery and personal ornaments; while a goodly sprinkl-
ing of silver and gold kneebuckles, shoebuckles, and
other such trinkets betrays the vanity with which the
colonial planter displayed his silk-stockinged calf and
shapely foot.[12]

Though there were practically no schools in the province it would be a gross error to infer from that fact
that the planters were either ignorant or illiterate
themselves or indifferent to the education of their
children. In infancy the children were taught at
home, but for their higher education they were sent to
Virginia, New England, and to the universities of
Scotland and England. "My principle desire," declared Wyriot Ormond, in his will, "is that of the
education of my daughters . . . and that no ex-
pense be thought too great." William Standin desired
that his son be taught "to read, rite and cifer as far
as the rule of three." Stephen Lee directed that his
son should be educated either in Philadelphia or Boston, while John Skinner provided for the education of
his son in North Carolina, "or other parts." Edward
Moseley directed that his sons should be sent elsewhere
when it became necessary to give them "other education that is to be had from the Common Masters in
this Province, for," he declared, "I would have my

---

12. See Grimes (editor): Abstracts of North Carolina
    Wills and also his North Carolina Wills and Inven-
    tories.

3

children well educated." These quotations from the
wills of the period are typical and might be continued
almost indefinitely.

Not so common, however, were such provisions as
that found in the will of John Baptista Ashe, in 1734,
which would do credit to the most modern professor of
pedagogy. "I will," said he, "that my slaves be kept
at work on my lands and that my estate be managed
to the best advantage so as my sons may have as
liberal an education as the profits thereof will afford; and in their education I pray my executors
to observe this method: Let them be taught to
read and write and be introduced into the practical
part of Arithmetick, not too hastily hurrying them to
Latin or Grammar; but after they are pretty well
versed in these, let them be taught Latin and Greek. I
propose this may be done in Virginia; after which let
them learn French; perhaps some Frenchman at San-
tee will undertake this. When they are arrived to
years of discretion let them study the Mathematicks.
To my sons when they arrive at age I recommend the
pursuit and study of some profession or business (I
could wish the one to ye Law, the other to Merchan-
dize), in which let them follow their own inclinations.
I will that my daughter be taught to write and read
and some feminine accomplishment which may render
her agreeable; and that she be not kept ignorant of
what appertains to a good housewife in the management of household affairs." [13]

There were of course no free public schools in the
province and while the planters as a rule provided only

---

13. Grimes (editor): North Carolina Wills and Inven-
    tories, 16-17.

for the education of those of their own households, it
was not an unknown thing for one to devote his wealth
to the education of the less fortunate. Thus as early as
1710 John Bennett, of Currituck county, left a portion
of his estate for the use of "poor old men and women
who have been honest and laborious," and another portion to "be for ye use & benefit of poor children to
pay for their schooling." [14] Better known is the
benefaction of James Winright, of Carteret county,
who in 1744 set aside the rents and profits of his lands
and houses in Beaufort "for the encouragement of a
sober discreet Qualified Man to teach school at Least
Reading, Writing, Vulgar and Decimal Arithmetick
in the aforesaid town of Beaufort."[15] Other evidences
of the education, culture and intelligence of the planters
are found in the books they read. Edward Moseley, as
is well known, established a free public library at Bath
in 1728, to which he donated £100 for the purchase of
books, most of which were in the Latin, Greek, and
Hebrew languages; while at his death he devised more
than four hundred volumes then in his private library.[16]
In the home of nearly every planter a few good books
were to be found, generally treatises on theology, moral
philosophy, law, history, and medicine. Among them
were the works of Sir Edward Coke, John Bunyan,
Increase Mathers, Richard Blome, Archbishop Tillot-
son, and other jurists, preachers, and theologians famous in their day and generation.[17]

If further evidence is needed of the character and
social standing of the planters of colonial Carolina it

---

14. Grimes (editor): North Carolina Wills and Inventories
16-17.
15. Ibid, 455.
16. Ibid, 313.
17. See especially the inventories printed in Grimes' Wills
and Inventories, p. 469 et seq.

is found in the general application to them of the term
"gentleman," then used as a class distinction, and in
their general use of such insignia as family crests and
coats-of-arms.   Says a scholarly Virginia historian:
"There is no reason to think that armorial bearings
were as freely and loosely assumed in those early times
as they are so often now, under Republican institutions; such bearings were then a right of property, as
clearly defined as any other, and continue to be in
modern England, what they were in colonial Virginia.
In the seventeenth century, when so large a proportion
of the persons occupying the highest position in the
society of the Colony were natives of England, the un-
warranted assumption of a coat-of-arms would proba-
bly have been as soon noticed, and perhaps as quickly
resented, as in England itself.   The prominent families
in Virginia were as well acquainted with the social
antecedents of each other in the Mother Country as
families of the same rank in England were with the
social antecedents of the leading families in the sur-
rounding shires; they were, therefore, thoroughly com-
petent to pass upon a claim of this nature; and the
fact that they were, must have had a distinct influence
in preventing a false claim from being put forward.
In a general way, it may be said it was quite as natural
for Virginians of those times to be as slow and care-
ful as contemporary Englishmen in advancing a claim
of this kind without a legal right on which to base it,
and, therefore, when they did advance it, that it was
likely to stand the test of examination by the numerous
persons in the colony who must have been familiar
with English coats-of-arms, in general. . . .   The
possession of coats-of-arms by the leading Virginian
families in the seventeenth century is disclosed in va-

rious incidental ways. Insignia of this kind are frequently included among the personal property ap-
praised in inventories. And they were also stampt on
pieces of fine silver plate."[18] A more frequent use
was as seals for letters and valuable papers. What
Mr. Bruce says of coats-of-arms in Virginia applies
with equal force in North Carolina. The great colonial families invariably sealed valuable papers with
seals bearing impression of their coats-of-arms.[19] They
prided themselves on their gentle blood and were extremely solicitous of the social position and dignity of
their families. They were men of culture and refine-
ment, thoroughly imbued with the political doctrines
of Hampden, Pym, and Eliot; and in the wild woods
of Carolina they became the political leaders of the
people, developing in their early struggles for self-gov-
ernment such leaders as George Durant, Thomas Pol-
lock, Edward Moseley, and Samuel Swann, the fore-
runners of the Harveys, the Harnetts, the Ashes, and
the Caswells of the Revolution.

The most important contributions made to our history and civilization by the English settlers in North
Carolina were political. To them we owe the form and
character of our government, and those great principles
of constitutional liberty upon which depend our peace,
prosperity, and happiness. They demanded that the
fundamental principles of the British Constitution in
its full vigor should follow them into their new home,
and they insisted that their charters should guarantee to them "all liberties, franchises and privileges" enjoyed by their fellow subjects in England. Without

---

18. Bruce: Social Life of Virginia in the Seventeenth Century, 105-108.
19. See Grimes' Abstract of North Carolina Wills, *passim.*

this guarantee we may be sure they would not have stirred an inch from the coast of Britain, and to it we owe all those safe-guards of our liberty,—representative government, the right of trial by jury, the privilege of the writ of *habeas corpus,* the principle that taxation without representation is tyranny, and all those other great constitutional principles which have for centuries characterized the governments of English-speaking peoples.   But though these principles were guaranteed by their charters the people of North Carolina were not permitted to enjoy them without a struggle.

In 1663, you will remember, the King granted Carolina to eight Lords Proprietors upon whom he conferred power to institute a government.[20]   Under this government the laws of the province were made by an Assembly chosen by the people, but they were administered by governors appointed by the Proprietors without the consent of the people.   The Proprietors were not always fortunate in their selection of the governors. Some were weak, some bad men, and but few cared anything for the people over whom they were sent to rule.   Indeed they were not the people's governors; they were the Proprietors' agents, and their first duty was to look out for the interests of their masters; when these interests conflicted with the welfare of the people, the latter and not the former was made to suffer.   Frequently, too, the governors were men of small abilities, puffed up with their importance, and inclined to run things with a high hand.   The result of course was continual clashing between the people and their rulers.

---

20. For the charters of 1663 and 1665 see Colonial Records of North Carolina, I, 20 and 102.

The former considering themselves entitled, by the terms of their charters, to "all the liberties, privileges and franchises" possessed by the people of England, and being too high-spirited to submit to the tyranny and insolence of the latter, more than once rose in revolt in defense of their liberties. Six Governors— Jenkins, Miller, Eastchurch, Sothel, Cary and Glover,— each in his turn, were either driven out or kept out of office by dominant factions of the irate people, who refused to see the charters of their liberties trampled under the feet of petty provincial officials. Indeed, in 1711 Governor Spotswood of Virginia declared that the people of Carolina were so used to turning their governors out of office that they had come to think they had a right to do so. Three times, too, with arms in their hands the stern, liberty-loving English farmers of Carolina rose in rebellion against violations of their constitutional rights: in the Culpepper Rebellion they resisted the enforcement of the navigation laws which they believed unconstitutionally interferred with their trade; in the Cary Rebellion they resisted the imposition of an oath of office which limited the right to sit in the Colonial Assembly to members of the Church of England because it restricted their political and religious freedom; in the Rent Riots they resisted the collection of illegal rents.

Historians taking a superficial view of these struggles and contests in the history of colonial Carolina have condemned those early Carolinians as a lawless and contentious people; but those who pronounce this judgment little understand the spirit which actuated them. When governed according to the terms of its charter no colony on the continent was more orderly or more law-abiding; on the other hand no people were ever more jealous of their constitutional rights or quicker to resent the encroachments of power. Adherence to their charter and resistance to its perversion were cardinal principles with North Carolinians throughout their colonial history; and their records are full of assertions of those principles on which the American Revolution was fought. As early as 1678 "when a few families were struggling into a consciousness of statehood along the wide waters of our eastern sounds," they declared that "the doctrine of non-resistance against arbitrary power and oppression is absurd, slavish and destructive to the good and happiness of mankind." In 1716 when the colony was but fifty years old and the population all told was less than ten thousand souls, the Assembly entered on its journal the declaration "that the impressing of the inhabitants, or their property, under pretence of its being for public service, without authority from the Assembly, was unwarrantable and a great infringement upon the liberty of the subject." Governor Burrington who spoke from the experience of ten years of residence among them wrote that the early Carolinians were "subtle and crafty to admiration." "The people," he declared, "are neither to be cajoled or outwitted; whenever a governor attempts to effect anything by these means he will lose his labour and show his ignorance. . . . They insist that no public money can or ought to be paid but by a claim given to and allowed by the house of burgesses." And John Urmstone, a missionary among them, declared that the people respected no authority that did not emanate from themselves. In a word, as Dr. Alderman has said: "The key to North Carolina character in this inchoate period is the subordination of everything—material prosper-

ity, personal ease, financial development,—to the re-
morseless assertion of the sacredness of chartered
rights" against the encroachments of the proprietary
government.[21]

The government of the Lords Proprietors was too
weak to afford any protection to the people or to preserve order in the province, yet it was strong enough
to be a source of constant irritation. When the great
war with the Indians, which nearly destroyed the
colony at a single blow, broke out in September 1711,
and when the pirates on the coast became so numerous,
so daring and so insolent as to threaten the colony
with ruin, it was not to the Lords Proprietors that the
people looked for aid, but to their sister colony of
South Carolina: nor did the Proprietors offer any assistance or protection. Yet the danger once past, and
peace restored, the hands of these rapacious overlords
fell heavily upon the exhausted resources of the province. The people of course were extremely restive
under a system which exacted much and yielded nothing, and the result was that neither they nor the Lords
Proprietors were satisfied with the experiment. Then,
too, King George regretted the prodigality with which
King Charles had given away such vast possessions
and conferred such extensive political power upon his
subjects. After sixty-five years of experimenting,
therefore, all parties were eager for a change, and
when the King in 1728, proposed to purchase the rights
of the Lords Proprietors, the suggestion found a hearty
welcome from both rulers and subjects. By this purchase North Carolina passed under the direct authority
of the Crown and the rule of the Lords Proprietors

---

21. William Hooper, p. 13.

came to an end. In North Carolina the change was celebrated with great public rejoicings.

The people had cause for their joy. Neglected by their rulers in time of danger, and nursed too attentively in time of peace and safety, what those early Carolinians had obtained they got through their own unassisted efforts and without favor from anybody. None of the colonies had passed through a more desperate struggle for existence, and none had had a more severe test of character and capacity. And can we not say too with all truth that none had borne the test better? What a gloomy picture of the condition of the people do we gather from the literature of the period immediately following the great Indian War of 1711-1715. The people have "scarcely corn to last them until wheat time, many not having any at all;" "the country miserably reduced by Indian cruelty;" "the inhabitants brought to so low an ebb that large numbers fled the province," "a country preserved which everybody that was but the least acquainted with our situation gave over for lost,"—these are typical expressions with which the letters of the period abound. That the colony survived these conditions is better evidence of the character and spirit of the people than the sneers and jibes of hostile critics, either contemporary or modern. Had the greater part of the population of North Carolina, or even a considerable minority of it, been composed of "the shiftless people who could not make a place for themselves in Virginia society," or "outlaws who fled [from Virginia] to escape the hangman," all the aristocracy of Virginia and South Carolina combined could not have saved the colony from anarchy and ruin. Yet between the years 1663 and 1728 somebody laid here in North Carolina the foundation of a great State. The foundation upon which great states are built is the character of their people, and the "mean whites" of Virginia are not now, nor were they then, the sort of people who found and build states. No colony composed to any extent of such a people could have rallied from such disasters as those from which North Carolina rallied between 1718 and 1728. Those years were years of growth and expansion. The population increased threefold; the Cape Fear was opened to settlers; new plantations were cleared; better methods of husbandry introduced; mills were erected; roads surveyed; ferries established; trade was increased; towns were incorporated; better houses built; better furniture installed; parishes were created; churches erected; ministers supplied; the schoolmaster found his way thither; and the colony was fairly started on that course of development which brought it by the outbreak of the Revolution to the rank of fourth in population and importance among the thirteen English-speaking colonies in America.

III

The Highland-Scotch in North Carolina

A range of mountains beginning in the county of Aberdeen and running in a southwesterly direction, divides Scotland into two distinct parts. The part lying to the south of the range is called the Lowlands; that to the north, the Highlands. The coastline of the Highlands is broken by long arms of the sea and bordered with groups of islands. The surface of the country, as its name implies, is mountainous. There is found some of the most beautiful scenery in the world. Tall rugged mountain peaks lifting their bare heads above soft green valleys, and sparkling streams hurrying to mingle their cool waters with the waters of innumerable glassy lakes, give a variety to the view that is never tiresome. Poets and musicians have celebrated the glories of the Highland in song and verse; and thousands of tourists, from the four corners of the world, annually pay tribute to its charm.

The Highlanders themselves are no less interesting than their country. Shut off for many ages from communication with the outside world by the rugged face of their mountains on the one side, and by their bold, rocky, and stormy coast on the other, they lived for one generation after another a life peculiar to themselves. The Highlanders knew but little of the Lowlanders, whom they thoroughly despised; and the Lowlanders knew but little of the Highlanders, whom they thoroughly feared. The former lived an outdoor life and engaged in occupations which required strength and courage and activity of mind and body. Following the chase over pathless mountains, waging constant war with their neighbors, and raiding the rich plains of the Lowlands were their principal pursuits. In this state of existence there was no place for the coward or the sluggard. Hardships and dangers were their daily portions, while the comforts, the luxuries, and the pleasures of civilized society were associated in their minds with cowardice and effeminacy. A natural consequence of this kind of life and these ideals was an enthusiastic admiration for physical beauty, strength and courage. As among all barbarous or semi-civilized people the weak and the puny perished; only the strong and the vigorous survived.

Legally and nominally the Highlanders were subjects of the King of Scotland, but in reality they paid to the royal authority such respect and yielded to it such obedience as suited their fancy. That loyalty which the people of other countries gave to their nation and to their king, the Highlanders gave to their clans and to their chiefs. The clan was composed of families tracing their descent from the same common ancestor, and bearing the same name. To guard the safety and the honor of the clan was the first duty of the clansman. An insult even to the humblest clansman by a member of another tribe was regarded as an insult to the whole clan. It was never forgotten nor forgiven, and if not avenged by one generation, it was handed down as a precious legacy to the next. Hence came that state of continuous warfare which existed in the Highlands.

At the head of each clan stood the chief, with whom every member of the clan claimed kinship. It was his duty to support his clansmen with his wealth and protect them with his power. Although theoretically subordinate to the will of the clan, he generally ruled over

it with "absolute and irresistible sway," and his commands were readily obeyed, "not from motives of fear,
but with the ready alacrity of confidence and affec-
tion." His clansmen obeyed his voice in their dealings
with each other; they rallied around him in his feuds
with neighboring chieftains; they followed his standard when he marched away to battle for the king.
When the chief called his clan to arms, the clansman
who failed to respond or lingered behind was branded
with infamy forever. The Highland chief counted his
wealth by the number of his followers. "How much is
your income?" an Englishman once asked the chief of
the MacDonalds. "I can raise five hundred men," was
the proud chief's laconic reply. The chief's pride in
his clan was equaled only by the clansman's devotion
to the person of his chief. For the safety, glory and
honor of his chief the true Highlander ever stood ready
to sacrifice all that he possessed. His own life he
counted as a worthless trifle when weighed in the
balance with that of his hereditary chieftain. Especial
emphasis is laid upon these facts because they were
the origin of the most striking and one of the most
admirable characteristics of the Highlander,—his un-
failing loyalty to his chief, his clan, and his cause.

To the isolation of their mountain homes and the
peculiarity of their social organization, we may add a
third potent influence which tended to keep the Highlanders a race apart,—their peculiar costume. The
Highlander's costume, as you well know, was as picturesque as his native hills. In a general way it consisted of a short coat, a vest, and a kilt, or "philabeg,"
which is a kind of petticoat reaching not quite to the
knees. The knees themselves were left bare, but the
lower part of the leg was covered with a short hose. A

belt encircled the waist and from it hung the "sporan," or pocket-purse, made of the skin of a goat or of a badger with the fur left on it. From the left shoulder, fastened by a brooch, hung the plaid or scarf, a piece of tartan two yards in breadth and four in length. The right, or sword arm, was left uncovered and at full liberty, and when both arms were needed the plaid was fastened across the breast by a large bodkin or brooch. In wet weather it was thrown loose so as to cover both the shoulders and the body. Each clan had a plaid of its own, differing in the combination of its colors from all others, so that a Campbell, or a MacDonald, or a MacLean could be known by his plaid. The costume was well adapted to the Highlander's mode of life. Its lightness and freedom permitted him to use his limbs and handle his arms with perfect ease. His arms, too, it may be said, formed part of his costume, for the Highlander was never without them. His weapons were a broad-sword, or "claymore," a dirk, and his trusty rifle. Before the introduction of fire-arms he wore a round shield on his left arm. The claymore had a long straight blade, a basket hilt, and was worn on the left side attached to a broad band which passed over the right shoulder. The dirk was a stouter and shorter weapon, intended for use in close quarters, and was worn on the right side. The sheath of the dirk was also provided with a hunting knife.

When a chief wished to summon his clansmen upon a sudden danger or for a sudden foray, he sent throughout his territory the Fiery Cross, or the "Cross of Shame." It was made by tying together two pieces of lightwood in the form of a cross. The ends of the cross were set on fire and after burning a little while, the burning ends were dipped in the blood of a goat slain

for the purpose. The burnt ends signified to the clansmen that the homes of all who failed to obey the call
of the chief would be given to the flames, the blood,
that he and all his family would be put to the sword.
It was sometimes called the "Cross of Shame," because disgrace forever followed the clansman who
failed or even hesitated to obey its message. The making of the cross was accomplished by elaborate cere-
monies, which closed when the old gray seer, or priest
of the clan, uttered his curse against

> . . . "the wretch who fails to rear
>   At this dread sign the ready spear.
> For, as the flames this symbol sear,
> His home—the refuge of his fear—
>   A kindred fate shall know;
> Far o'er its roof the volumed flame
> Clan-Alpine's vengeance shall proclaim,
> While maids and matrons on his name
> Shall call down wretchedness and shame,
>   And infamy and woe."

A swift and trusty messenger then snatched the
"dread sign" from the feeble hands of the seer, dashed
away over the mountains and across the streams, showing it to every clansman, naming the time and the
meeting-place. At the sight of the Fiery Cross every
man in the clan must instantly snatch his weapons and
hasten with all the speed possible to obey the call of
his chief. No excuse answered for delay: the son must
leave his dying father; the bridegroom his weeping
bride, for before all other duties came the duty to the
clan and loyalty to the chief. One messenger after
another took charge of the fatal sign, until with great
speed it had gone throughout the territory of the clan.

In war the chief led his clansmen in person. Every clan had its battle-cry and its war-song. At the battle of Moore's Creek Bridge, where members of several clans fought under MacDonald, their battle-cry was, "King George and broadswords!" His great physical strength, his long training, his daring impetuosity, and his scorn of death, made the Highlander terrible in battle; but his habits of life made him a poor soldier for an extended campaign. When a battle was over, the campaign, in his opinion, was ended; if it was lost, he sought safety in his mountains; if won, he returned thither to secure his booty. In either case he was ready to go home, and this habit often rendered the most complete victory fruitless, and made the Highlander a troublesome ally on an extended campaign; the general never knew when he might suddenly find himself without an army.

Such were the Highlanders in their native country. When they came to North Carolina to live they brought many of their customs and peculiar habits and beliefs with them. Their emigration to this country began about the middle of the eighteenth century, and from that time until the outbreak of the Revolution the flow from the Highlands of Scotland to North Carolina continued in an almost unbroken stream. There was something very extraordinary about this movement, for the Highlander, deeply devoted to his own country, seldom stirred abroad and never undertook the conquest of foreign territory with a view to permanent occupancy. His natural home was in the Highlands and his devotion to it was strengthened by his intense loyalty to his clan and to his chief. Death was much to be preferred to exile and for the true Highlander death itself lost half its terrors if he felt

4

assured that his body was to rest beneath his native sod. It is interesting, therefore, to seek an explanation of their remarkable emigration to America during the eighteenth century. The explanation is found in two closely related causes, both the outgrowth of their peculiar industrial and social systems: first, agricultural conditions in the Highlands; secondly, their political misfortunes.

The structure of Highland society rested upon a military basis. In the dealings of one clan with another "Might made right," and accordingly the importance of any clan depended upon the number of armed men that it could rally to the standard of its chief. The natural result of this system, of course, was that the Highlander was trained to the use of the claymore and the dirk rather than the plow and the sickle. Tilling and reaping were no proper employment for warriors, and agricultural labor fell upon the shoulders of the women and the weaklings of the clan. Their country, naturally rocky and barren, would yield but a meagre support even when in a high state of cultivation, but their agriculture was on the most limited scale and their fields were cultivated in the simplest manner and with the rudest tools. Nor was their trade any better: except the occasional sale of a drove of cattle, too frequently driven from the pasture of some Lowland laird without so much as a "by your leave," they had no trade. It follows of course that there were no manufactures and no commerce. That genius and energy which the people of other countries had learned to devote to the arts and the sciences of peace, the Highlanders were still devoting, even as late as the eighteenth century, to the arts of war and the chase. The inevitable result of this system was that many of the clans counted more clansmen than their lands could possibly support. To add further to the suffering caused by these conditions, the British Government, after the battle of Culloden in 1746, determined to break up the clan system, confiscated the hereditary estates of the chiefs, and distributed their lands to British soldiers. These new landlords, caring nothing for the welfare of the Highlanders, and finding sheep-raising more profitable than farming, turned into pasture-lands thousands of acres which theretofore had always been under cultivation. This change, as it required fewer people to raise sheep than to cultivate the land, inevitably added to the general distress. Rents increased, hundreds of families were deprived of their means of livelihood, and the complete overthrow of their social and industrial systems left them helpless.

The other cause of their emigration to America was their political misfortunes. As head of the royal family of Scotland, the reigning prince of the House of Stuart was regarded by many of the Highland clans as their common chief. However much they might quarrel among themselves most of the clans owned allegiance to the Stuarts and when the members of that unhappy family, after years of misrule in England, were finally expelled from that kingdom by the long-suffering English people, they appealed to the loyalty of their Highland clans for support in their efforts to regain the throne. To such an appeal from their hereditary chieftains, whatever their faults and vices might be, the Scottish clansmen had but one answer, and for more than half a century they clung to the fortunes of the fallen Stuarts with a loyalty and devotion deserving of a better cause. Their last attempt to recover the throne

for that unhappy family was made in 1746. In the
early part of the winter Prince Charles Stuart, the
"Young Pretender," who had been raised an exile in
France, landed on the shores of Scotland and called
upon the Highlanders to join him in an invasion of
England. The Fiery Cross was dispatched throughout
the Highlands, the clansmen responded with true Highland enthusiasm, and soon every hall and vale in the
Highlands was resounding with the clash of arms and
echoing with the popular chorus,

> We'll o'er the water, we'll o'er the sea,
> We'll o'er the water to Charlie!
> Come weal, come woe, we'll gather and go,
> And live and die wi' Charlie!

At first the impetus of their enthusiasm swept everything before them, and Charles Stuart saw visions of a
crown dangling within his grasp. But from that un-
speakable calamity the English nation was saved, on
April 16, 1746, when with great slaughter the Highlanders were swept from the field of Culloden, and
Charles Stuart, glad to exchange the royal ermine for
the petticoat of an Irish waiting maid, was saved from
the block by the devoted loyalty and romantic daring
of Flora MacDonald.

The British Government now determined to visit the
Highlanders with such severity as to make future rebellion impossible. The authority of the chiefs over
their clansmen was abolished, their estates were confiscated, and the carrying of arms and the wearing of
the tribal costumes were made crimes punishable
with great severity. An English army under the Duke
of Cumberland, forever afterwards known in Highland
history as "Butcher Cumberland," established head-

quarters at the town of Inverness, and from this base, his soldiers fell upon the helpless inhabitants throughout the Highlands and laid waste their country for miles in every direction. Their cattle were driven away or slaughtered; the mansions of the chiefs and the huts of the clansmen were laid in ashes; captured Highland soldiers were put to death with brutal ferocity; women and children, without food, without homes, without husbands and fathers, wandered helplessly among the hills and valleys to die of cold and hunger. It became the boast of the English soldiery that neither house nor cottage, man nor beast could be found within fifty miles of Inverness: all was silence, ruin, and desolation unparalleled in modern warfare until Sherman marched through Georgia.

Driven from their ancient estates, subjected to the wanton insults and cruelties of a brutal soldiery, and forbidden to observe the social customs of their ancestors, thousands of the Highlanders turned their eyes toward America as their only haven of freedom, prosperity, and happiness. As early as 1729 a few families of Highlanders had settled on the Cape Fear River in North Carolina. There they found a genial climate, a fertile soil, and a mild and liberal government. Everything contributed to their happiness and contentment, and their letters to friends and relatives in Scotland glowed with praise of their new home. Five years later, 1734, Gabriel Johnston, a Scotchman inordinately fond of his countrymen, became governor of the colony, and throughout his long administration exerted himself to spread the fame of North Carolina throughout the Highlands. Consequently when Neal McNeal, one of the earliest of the Scotch settlers on the Cape Fear, visited Scotland in 1739, carrying tidings of the new land beyond the Atlantic, he found a fertile soil in which to sow his seed, and upon his return to North Carolina in the autumn, brought a ship-load of 350 Highlanders. They landed at Wilmington where according to tradition their peculiar costume and outlandish language so frightened the town officials that they attempted to make the strangers take an oath to keep the peace, but from this indignity McNeal managed to save them, and taking his countrymen up the river to the Highland settlement, found for them there a hearty welcome. At the session of the Assembly in February, 1740, Dugal McNeal and McAllister, presented a petition in behalf of these immigrants in which they stated "if proper encouragement be given them, that they'l invite the rest of their friends and acquaintances over;" and the House of Commons passed a series of resolutions exempting the petitioners from taxation for ten years; appropriating £1,000 for their subsistence; exempting all such immigrants, who came in companies numbering as many as forty each, from taxation for ten years after their arrival; and requesting the governor to use his influence to encourage others to come. The Council, however, deferred action on these resolutions till the next Assembly but failed then to take them up for consideration.[1] The action of the House is of interest chiefly as showing the favorable attitude of the colony toward these Highland-Scotch settlers. On the heels of this liberal action came the disaster of Culloden, the rise in rents, and the harsh enactments of the British Parliament, and immediately a flow of population from the Highlands

---

1. Colonial Records, IV, 489-490.

to the New World set in so strong and steady that the refrain of one of the popular songs of the day was,

"Going to seek a fortune in North Carolina."[2]

Shipload after shipload of sturdy Highland settlers reached the shores of America, and most of them landing at Charleston and Wilmington found their way to their kinsmen on the Cape Fear. Here in a few years their settlements were thickly scattered throughout the territory now embraced in the counties of Anson, Bladen, Cumberland, Harnett, Moore, Richmond, Robeson, Sampson, Scotland, and Hoke. With a keen appreciation of its commercial advantages they selected a point of land at the head of navigation on the Cape Fear where they laid out a town, first called Campbellton, then Cross Creek, and finally Fayetteville.

The Highlanders continued to pour into North Carolina right up to the outbreak of the Revolution, but as no official record of their numbers was kept it is impossible to say how numerous they were. Perhaps, however, from reports in the periodicals, letters, and other documents of the day, we may arrive at some idea of their numerical importance. In 1755 it was estimated that there were in Bladen county about 500 white persons, most of whom were Highlanders, capable of bearing arms, from which it is reasonable to infer that the total population was not less than 2,500. The *Scots Magazine,* in September 1769, records that the ship *Molly* had recently sailed from Islay filled with passengers for North Carolina, and that this was the third emigration from that county within six years.

---

2. The Gaelic is:
    Dol a ah 'iarruidh an fhortain do North Carolina.

The same journal in a later issue tells us that between April and July, 1770, fifty-four vessels sailed from the Western Isles laden with 1,200 Highlanders all bound for North Carolina. Two years later the ship *Adventure* bore a cargo of 200 emigrants from the Highlands to the Cape Fear, and in March of the same year Governor Martin wrote to Lord Hillsborough, Secretary of State for the Colonies; "Near a thousand people have arrived in Cape Fear River from the Scottish Isles since the month of November with a view to settling in this province whose prosperity and strength will receive great augmentation by the accession of such a number of hardy, laborious and thrifty people." In 1773 the *Courant,* another Scottish paper, declared that 800 people from Skye had already engaged a vessel to take them to their kinsmen in North Carolina. The ship *Jupiter* sailed in 1775 with 200 emigrants bound for the same colony, and as late as October of that year, after the Revolution was well under way, Governor Martin notes the arrival at Wilmington of a shipload of 172 Highlanders. From 1769 to 1775 the Scotch journals mention as many as sixteen different emigrations besides "several others." Not all of these emigrants came to North Carolina. Georgia, New York, Canada, and other colonies received a small share, but "the earliest, largest and most important settlement of Highlanders in America, prior to the Peace of 1783, was in North Carolina along Cape Fear River."[3] Governor Martin wrote to the King in 1775, that he could raise in this colony an army of 3,000 Highlanders, from which it is a reason-

---

3. MacLean: The Highlanders in America, p. 102.   See also
    Hanna: The Scotch-Irish in America.

able conclusion that at that time the Highland-Scotch population of North Carolina was not less than 15,000. Several of the clans were represented, but at the outbreak of the Revolution the MacDonalds so largely predominated in numbers and in leadership that the campaign of 1776, which ended at Moore's Creek Bridge, was spoken of at the time as the "insurrection of the Clan MacDonald."

Though unfortunate economic conditions lay behind this Highland emigration, it is not therefore to be supposed that those who left their native land to seek homes in America belonged to an improvident and thriftless class, or that they arrived in Carolina emptyhanded. Such people, as was pointed out in the lecture on the English, are not the kind of people who voluntarily take upon their shoulders the task of conquering the wilderness and laying the foundations of great states and governments. The Highland emigrants were among the most substantial and energetic people of Scotland and they left the land of their nativity because it did not offer them an outlet for their activities. The *Scots Magazine* in 1771 tells us that a band of 500 of these emigrants had recently sailed for America "under the conduct of a gentleman of wealth and merit, whose ancestors had resided in Islay for many centuries past." Another colony, according to the same journal, was composed of "the most wealthy and substantial people in Skye," while the *Courant,* in 1773, declared that a colony of nearly 500 emigrants who had just sailed were, "the finest set of fellows in the Highlands," and that they carried "at least £6,000 sterling in ready cash with them." From the single county of Sunderland, in 1772 and 1773, about 1,500 emigrants sailed for America, who, according to the *Courant,*

carried with them an average of £4 sterling to the
man. "This," says that journal, "amounts to £7,500
which exceeds a year's rent of the whole county." It
is not so easy to arrive at any satisfactory conclusion
as to the financial condition of the Highlanders after
their arrival in North Carolina. On the whole they
were poor when compared with their English neighbors, but their condition was undoubtedly a great
improvement over what it had been in Scotland.

From both the Governor and the Assembly as well
as the people generally, the Highlanders received numerous evidences of welcome to their adopted country.
As early as 1740 the Governor commissioned several of
their leading men justices of the peace. In 1758
Hector McNeill was appointed sheriff of Cumberland
county, but the services of a sheriff seem not to have
been greatly in demand, for McNeill's fees for the
whole year amounted to only ten pounds. By 1754 the
Highland settlement around Campbellton had grown
so important that the General Assembly erected it
into a county which, with curious irony, was called in
honor of "Butcher Cumberland," and gave it the privilege of sending two representatives to the Assembly. A
few years later the Assembly passed an act providing
for the building of a road from the river Dan on the
Virginia line through the counties of Guilford, Chat-
ham and Cumberland to Cross Creek on the Cape Fear,
and another leading to it from Shallow Ford in Surry
county. Thus Cross Creek became the trading point
for all the back country as far inland as the Moravian
settlement around Salem, and soon grew into one of
of the principal towns in the province.

The Highlanders desired to reproduce in Carolina
the life they had lived in Scotland, but changed condi-

tions, as they soon found, made this impossible. True no law made it illegal for the clans to maintain their tribal organizations, or forbade the chiefs to exercise their hereditary authority, or made it a crime for the clansmen to bear arms, or to wear the tartan. But as the basis of the clan system was military necessity, in the absence of such necessity the system could not flourish. In Scotland the clansmen had obeyed their chief in return for his protection against hostile neighbors; in Carolina there were no hostile neighbors, Law reigned supreme, and under its benign sway the humblest clansman was assured of far more effective protection of life and property than the most powerful chief in the Highlands could possibly have given him. As soon as the clan system became unnecessary it became irksome and irritating, and rapidly disappeared. With its passing passed also the meaning, and therefore the usefulness, of the Highland costume, which was soon laid aside for the less picturesque but more serviceable dress of their English fellow countrymen. Their language was destined to a similar fate. When preaching in English to the Highlanders at Cross Creek in 1756 Hugh McAden found that many of them "scarcely knew one word" he spoke. The Gaelic made a brave struggle against the all-conquering English tongue, but a vain and useless one. Entrenched in an impregnable stronghold as the language of all legal, social, political and commercial transactions, English effected an easy conquest, and the Gaelic speech disappeared as a common medium of expression, surviving only among a few ancient fathers who, lingering beyond the alloted time, found it a convenient language in which to glorify the splendors of the past and bemourn the degeneracy of their own day. Under these circumstances the peculiar political and social institutions of the Highlanders gave way before those of their adopted country, and after the second generation of Highland settlers had followed their fathers to the grave nothing remained to distinguish their descendants from their English countrymen save only their Highland names.

The Highlanders were peculiarly unfortunate in the time at which they came to America. Nothing could have been more essential to their welfare than peace and quiet, freedom from political agitation and from the calamities of war. But for them there seemed to be no peace, and in exchanging Scotland for Carolina they seemed but to have exchanged the character of their troubles. From 1768 to 1771, the period during which the greater part of them reached our shores, civil war raged in North Carolina between the colonial government and the Regulators. In this much misunderstood event the sympathies of the Highlanders seem to have been wholly on the side of law and order, and when Governor Tryon marched against the rebels in 1771 a company of Highlanders under Captain Farquard Campbell fought bravely under his command at Alamance.

The outbreak of the Revolution presented to the Highlanders a far more momentous question. Should they array themselves under the royal standard and support the cause of established government, or should they again risk all upon the uncertain venture of rebellion and revolution? If we find that the Highlanders, when brought face to face with so important a problem, rendered the wrong decision, let us recall their recent experience in Scotland and the circumstances under which they emigrated to the New World before we presume to pronounce judgment. At the beginning of the disputes with the mother country, when nobody dreamed of any other action on the part of the colonists than the presentation of legal and peaceful petitions and protests, the sympathies of the Highlanders on the whole were with their fellow colonists. Hardly had they become settled on the Cape Fear when those peaceful waters were disturbed by the outbreaks at Brunswick and Wilmington which speedily followed the passage of the Stamp Act. It was not to be expected of course that the Highlanders should take any part in this resistance, but so far as they showed any interest at all it was against the Ministry. At Cross Creek Lord Bute, the favorite of George III, who was supposed to be the moving spirit behind the passage of the Stamp Act, was burned in effigy, and a letter written from that place to the patriots of Wilmington called upon them in the name of "dear liberty" to resist any attempt to land the stamps in North Carolina. In 1775 and 1776 the Highlanders sent Farquard Campbell, Thomas Rutherford, Alexander McKay, and Alexander MacAlister, all good Highland names, to represent them in the provincial congresses and they also had their committees of safety.

But when they saw that these congresses and committees were drifting toward open rebellion and war, they refused to follow. Thereupon the Provincial Congress appointed a committee made up principally of Highlanders who had long been residents of the colony "to confer with the gentlemen who have lately arrived from the Highlands in Scotland to settle in this Province, and to explain to them the nature of our unhappy controversy with Great Britain, and to advise and urge them to unite with the other inhabitants of America in defense of those rights which they derive from God and the Constitution."[4]   But this mission was in vain: the Highlanders were willing to petition the King and Parliament for a redress of their grievances, but they would not take up arms against the Crown; the truth is they had had enough of rebellion in Scotland and they showed no inclination to repeat the experiment in America.   Consequently when the appeal to arms came the Highlanders withdrew their support from the Revolutionary party and indicated to the Governor their willingness to support the royal cause.

The most influential of the Highland leaders was Allan MacDonald, husband of the famous Flora MacDonald, a man of great dignity, stately bearing, and noble, impressive countenance.   Him and his son-in-law, Alexander McLeod, the royal governor, Martin, recommended to the King for appointment as major and captain, respectively, saying of them, "besides being men of great worth and good character, [they] have most extensive influence over the Highlanders here, a great part of whom are of their own names and families."   MacDonald, so lately in rebellion against the House of Hanover, was now eager to make a display of his loyalty, and in July, 1775, he paid a secret visit to Governor Martin to perfect with him plans for organizing and arming his countrymen.   Their plans met with the hearty concurrence of the King and Ministry, and had a most important bearing on the fate of the American cause in the South.   Briefly, they were as follows: MacDonald was to organize and arm the Highlanders and march them to Wilmington, where

---

4. Colonial Records, X, 173.

they were to be joined by Lord Cornwallis with seven regiments of British regulars, escorted by a powerful fleet of fifty-two sails under the command of Sir Peter Parker. Sir Henry Clinton with a force of 2,000 troops from the British army at Boston was to sail for Wilmington and take command of the expedition. It was fully expected that before such a combined force North Carolina would fall an easy victim, and then could be used as a base for operations against South Carolina, Georgia, and Virginia, thus cutting off the entire South from the middle and northern colonies and crushing the rebellion at its very inception.

That this scheme did not succeed was due to the splendid victory of the Whigs at Moore's Creek Bridge in the early morning hours of February 27, 1776. Here was an event of far greater significance than is usually accorded to it in our histories, and the historian Frothingham is guilty of no exaggeration when he calls it the "Lexington and Concord" of the South. The first day of February, 1776, was set as the date for the gathering of the clans, and on that day the royal standard was unfurled at Cross Creek. The Fiery Cross had been sent abroad, and soon the clansmen gathered from far and near, "from the wide plantations on the river bottoms, and from the rude cabins in the depths of the lonely pine forests, with broadswords at their sides, in tartan garments and feathered bonnets, and keeping step to the shrill music of the bag-pipe. There came, first of all, Clan Mac-Donald with Clan MacLeod near at hand, with lesser numbers of Clan MacKensie, Clan MacRae, Clan Mac-Lean, Clan MacKay, Clan MacLachlan, and still others —variously estimated at from fifteen hundred to three thousand."[5] Drawn up in battle array, this Highland host presented a martial spectacle that might have stirred the sluggish blood of King George himself; and cheer after cheer broke from the throats of the loyal clansmen as their beloved Flora MacDonald, the pride of every true Highlander, gracefully seated on a milk-white horse,[6] rode down their line and called upon them to do battle loyally for their sovereign and his crown.

On February 18th the Highlanders, 1,600 strong, singing the songs of their native hills and keeping step to the music of the bag-pipes, marched out of Cross Creek and took the road to Wilmington. After some marching and counter-marching, they reached the bridge over Moore's Creek late in the evening of February 26, and there encamped for the night. Beyond the bridge 1,100 sturdy Whigs, under Colonel Richard Caswell and Colonel Alexander Lillington, slept upon their arms, waiting the command to dispute the passage with the MacDonalds. The sun had not yet risen behind the dark and sombre pines on the morning of the twenty-seventh, when the Scots broke camp and prepared for battle. Their signal for attack was to be three cheers, the drums to beat and the pipes to play; their battle cry was "King George and broadswords." Leading the way Donald MacLeod stepped upon the bridge and called on his men to follow. From out of the dark beyond a voice rang out in the cold, crisp air: "Who goes there?" "A friend," replied MacLeod. "A friend to whom?" demanded the other. "To the King," answered the Scot. Then fell a deathly silence,

---

5. MacLean: The Highlanders in America, p. 127.
6. Tradition.

suddenly broken by the loud report of a gun, as Mac-
Leod shouted the signal for attack, and dashed upon
the bridge, followed by his men. The American mus-
kets laid the brave Highlander low, and swept the
bridge clear of his followers. Others rushed into the
breach, but in vain. Thirty of the foremost fell dead,
the rest lost heart, turned and fled. No victory could
be more complete. The patriots had but one man
killed and one wounded; the total killed among the
Highlanders was about seventy, and their army was
completely scattered. Three hundred and fifty guns,
150 swords and dirks, 1,500 excellent rifles, a box containing £15,000 in gold, thirteen wagons of supplies,
850 soldiers and many officers including Allan Mac-
Donald, fell into the hands of the victors. A few days
later Clinton and Cornwallis sailed into the Cape Fear
with their powerful fleet and army, but no loyalist
force was there to welcome them. Abandoning an
enterprise so desperately begun they sailed away to
Charleston to knock in vain against the palmetto logs
of Fort Moultrie.

The victory at Moore's Creek Bridge saved North
Carolina from conquest, and in all probability saved
Virginia, South Carolina, and Georgia to the American cause. Of this victory Bancroft writes: "In less
than a fortnight, more than nine thousand four hundred men of North Carolina rose against the enemy;
and the coming of Clinton inspired no terror. . . .
Virginia offered assistance, and South Carolina would
gladly have contributed relief; but North Carolina had
men enough of her own to crush insurrection and
guard against invasion; and as they marched in
triumph through their piney forests, they were per-
suaded that in their own woods they could win an easy

5

victory over British regulars. The terrors of a fate
like that of Norfolk could not dismay the patriots of
Wilmington; the people spoke more and more of independence; and the Provincial Congress, at its im-
pending session, was expected to give an authoritative
form to the prevailing desire."[7]   The Provincial Congress met at Halifax April 4, 1776, and eight days
later, April 12, "Resolved, that the delegates for this
Colony in the Continental Congress be impowered to
concur with the delegates of the other Colonies in declaring Independency, and forming foreign alliances."
Thus as a result of their brilliant victory over the
Highlanders, "the patriot party" in the words of
Richard Frothingham, "carried North Carolina as a
unit in favor of independence, when the colonies from
New England to Virginia were in solid array against
it."[8]

The fate of the Highlanders was a hard one. In
1777, the General Assembly determined that the safety
of the State demanded the expulsion from its borders
of all who would not take the oath of allegiance. Accordingly an act was passed which held out to all
Loyalists the alternative of allegiance or banishment.
True to their principles, most of those who were Loyalists from conviction accepted the latter choice. Chief
among them were the Scotch-Highlanders who de-
parted in large numbers. "Two-thirds of Cumberland
county intend leaving this State," reported the colonel
of the militia of that county in July, 1777. "Great
Numbers of these infatuated and over-loyal People,"
said the *North Carolina Gazette*, in October, 1777,

---

7. History of the United States, (edition of 1860), VIII.,
   289-290.
8. Rise of the Republic of the United States, p. 504.

"returned from America to their own Country," among whom was Flora MacDonald. Others found new homes in Nova Scotia. Among the prominent Highlanders who left North Carolina in 1777 was John Hamilton, "a merchant of considerable note," who sailed from New Bern on a "Scotch transport, having on Board a Number of Gentlemen of that Nation." Hamilton afterwards organized these Highlanders into a Loyalist regiment which on numerous battlefields in the South worthily maintained the high reputation of their race for its fighting qualities. This exodus of the Highlanders from North Carolina in 1777 was comparable to their exodus from Scotland after Culloden. The policy which was responsible for it was perhaps the only course open to the new State; nevertheless one may be permitted to regret that circumstances compelled North Carolina to drive from her borders so many men and women of this strong, virile race.

It was the peculiar misfortune of the Highlanders to suffer defeat in Scotland fighting against the House of Hanover, and again to suffer defeat in America fighting for the House of Hanover. In either case, however much we may lament their error of judgment, we cannot fail to applaud their sense of loyalty to duty as they understood it. That same sense of loyalty led those who remained after the Revolution to pledge their allegiance to their new country in whose service their descendants have always manifested an equal readiness to labor and to sacrifice. In every department of our government descendants of the Highlanders have rendered distinguished service, and in every crisis of our history they have been conspicuous for prompt and ready response to the call of duty. To estimate correctly how much North Carolina is in-

debted to this race, let us recall in military history the
names of Charles and Joseph McDowell, whose daring
deeds on the very crest of King's Mountain turned the
tide of the Revolution and led the way to Yorktown;
in constitutional history the names of Samuel Johnston and Archibald Maclaine, whose ability and learning contributed so largely to the formation of the State
Constitution of 1776 and to the ratification of the Fed-
eral Constitution by North Carolina; in politics the
names of James J. McKay, for many years the leader
of his party in the National Congress; in jurispru-
dence James C. McRae and Robert M. Douglas, succes-
sors of Gaston and Ruffin on the Supreme Court Bench;
in industry Paul C. Cameron; in literature John
Charles McNeill; in education Charles Duncan McIver
—Highland names all, which remind us that in their
contributions to the history and fame of North Carolina the Highlanders have been second to no element in
our population.

IV

The Scotch-Irish in North Carolina

During the four decades from 1735 to 1775 two streams of population flowing mostly from Pennsylvania poured into the central part of North Carolina and spread far and wide over the fertile plains and valleys of that section. Though flowing side by side these streams originated in separate sources and throughout their courses kept themselves entirely distinct. One was composed of immigrants of German descent, the other of immigrants of Scotch-Irish descent. Today we are concerned only with the latter.

The term Scotch-Irish is a misnomer, and does not, as one would naturally suppose, signify a mixed race of Scotch and Irish ancestry. It is a geographical, not a racial term. Those who proudly claim this name reject with ill-founded disdain the implication conveyed by the latter half of the compound, and point with justifiable pride to their pure Scottish descent. The so-called Scotch-Irish are in reality Scotch people, or descendants of Scotch people who once resided in Ireland. Into that country they came as invaders and lived as conquerors, hated as such by the natives, and feeling for them the contempt which conquerors always feel for subjugated races. From one generation to another the two races dwelt side by side separated by an immense chasm of religious, political, social, and racial hostility, each intent upon preserving its blood pure and uncontaminated by any mixture with the other. Thus the Scotch in Ireland remained Scotch, and the term "Irish" as applied to them is nothing more than a geographical term used to distinguish the

Scotch immigrants who came to America from Ireland from those who came hither directly from Scotland. In fact the term "Scotch-Irish" is American in its origin and use, and is not known or used in Ireland. In that country, whose Irish population is almost entirely Roman Catholic in religion, the descendants of the Scotch settlers are generally known as "Irish Protestants" or "Irish Presbyterians." This is a far more significant term than our "Scotch-Irish." It raises the natural and inevitable inquiry, Whence came they? It recalls their long and bitter struggle for existence against the native population. It points to the ardor, the depth, the sincerity of their religious faith. It testifies to their force of character and their intellectual vigor. They are, as the name tells us, Protestants in Ireland; hence their presence there must be explained. They are the representatives of Presbyterianism in the very stronghold of Catholicism; hence we may infer a long and bitter struggle for the right to exist with its ultimate victory. They are distinguished from the general population by a religious term, hence we may know that they are earnest, immovable, sincere in their religious convictions. They have in the face of intense religious and racial antagonism remained firm, fearless, triumphant over overwhelming numbers; hence we deduce their strength of character and keenness of intellect. A people possessing such marked characteristics are evidently well worthy of serious study.

The Scotch settlers of Ireland came principally from the Lowlands of Scotland. This region lies to the south and west of the river Clyde and in area is about one-tenth the size of North Carolina. It is perhaps not too much to say that no other region of the same size in the modern world has produced a larger number of eminent men. "It is only necessary," says Dr. McKelway, "to mention the names of William Wallace, Robert Bruce, John Knox, and Robert Burns to show that the race that inhabited these western Lowlands was a virile race. Here arose the royal line of the Stuarts; the family of which William Ewart Gladstone was the most illustrious scion; and the ancestors of our own Washington. Here lived the Lollards, Reformers before the Reformation, and here were marshalled the leaders and armies of the Reformation itself. Here was the chief home of the Covenanters. Here has been built the great manufacturing city of the modern world, Glasgow, a model city in many respects. And from these seven counties flowed the main stream of immigrants into the province of Ulster, Ireland, from which they emigrated in turn to the American colonies, to be known henceforth as Scotch-Irish."[1]

A fine description of the Lowland Scotch has been drawn by Senator Henry Cabot Lodge. Says he: "It is a remarkable history, that of Scotland, one of the most remarkable in the annals of men. Shut up in that narrow region of mountain and of lake, a land of storm and cold and mist, with no natural resources except a meager soil and a tempestuous sea to yield a hard-earned living; poor in this world's goods, few in number, for six hundred years these hardy people maintained their independence against their powerful foe to the southward, and only united at last upon equal terms. For six hundred years they kept their place among the nations, were the allies of France,

---

1. McKelway: The Scotch-Irish in North Carolina (*N. C. Booklet*, Vol. IV, No. 11).

were distinguished for their military virtues on the
continent of Europe, and cherished a pride of race
and country to which their deeds gave them an un-
clouded title. They did all these things, this little people, by hard fighting. For six hundred years they
fought, sometimes in armies, sometimes in bands, always along the border, frequently among themselves.
It was a terrible training. It did not tend to promote
the amenities of life, but it gave slight chance to the
timid or the weak. Those six centuries of bitter struggle for life and independence, waged continuously
against nature and man, not only made the Scotch
formidable in battle, renowned in every camp in
Europe, but they developed qualities of mind and character which became inseparable from the race. For it
was not merely by changing blows that the Scotch
maintained their national existence. Under the stress
of all these centuries of trial they learned to be patient
and persistent, with a fixity of purpose which never
weakened, a tenacity which never slackened, and a determination which never wavered. The Scotch intellect, passing through the same severe ordeal, as it was
quickened, tempered, and sharpened, so it acquired a
certain relentlessness in reasoning which it never lost.
It emerged at last complete, vigorous, acute, and penetrating. With these strong qualities of mind and character was joined an intensity of conviction which
burned beneath the cool and calculating manner of
which the stern and unmoved exterior gave no sign,
like the fire of a furnace, rarely flaming, but giving
forth a fierce and lasting heat."[2]

---

2. Address in the U. S. Senate, March 12, 1910, at the pre-
    sentation to the United States by the State of South
    Carolina of a statue of John C. Calhoun.

The three characteristics which have most distinguished the Scotch-Irish are: (1) The earnestness of their religious convictions; (2) their democracy; (3) their interest in education.

(1) In estimating the character of the Lowland Scotch, the most important fact to be considered is their religion. To it we may trace in a large measure that intensity of conviction, that tenacity of purpose, that vigor of intellect of which Senator Lodge so eloquently speaks. The Scotch Lowlander was an intellectual, not an emotional being, and his religious faith was founded on intellectual convictions rather than on spiritual emotions. To his type of intellect, penetrating, logical, delighting in abstractions, the theology of Calvin and Knox appealed with especial force, and having once embraced their doctrines he was prepared to follow the Calvinistic logic to its ultimate conclusions. Forced to battle for existence not only against Roman Catholicism, but also against the Protestant Church of England, the Scotch Calvinists became the Protestants of Protestantism. Their system of Presbyterianism grew up at the outset without direct recognition from the law. It bound Scotland together as it had never been bound before, by its administrative organization, its Church synods and general assemblies, and by the power which it gave the lay elders in each congregation. It summoned the laymen in an overwhelming majority to the earlier assemblies, and thus called the people at large to a decisive voice in the administration of affairs. "No Church constitution," says John Richard Greene, "has proved in practice so democratic as that of Scotland." Its influence raised the nation at large to a consciousness of its own power, for the sphere of action to which it called the people

was in fact not a mere ecclesiastical but a national sphere; and the power of the Church was felt more and more in the political affairs of the nation. Indeed, the Scottish people rose into power under the guise of the Scottish Kirk.

(2) Their democracy not only in ecclesiastical but in political affairs as well. Calvinism exalted the individual man, and accordingly the Church which grew out of it was a democratic institution, resting upon the individual. Each congregation sent representatives to the synods and to the assemblies. The Church, therefore, legislated for itself, not through bishops and clergy, but through the laymen, that is, the people, and this is the very essence of democracy. Now, in a country where Church and State are so closely allied as they were in Scotland in the sixteenth century, it is but a short step from ecclesiastical to political affairs. The same democratic principles, therefore, which prevailed in the Church might easily be made to prevail in the State. Thus the Scottish Presbytery became a training school for democracy. No one understood this better than King James. "A Scottish Presbytery," he declared, "as well fitteth with monarchy as God and the Devil. No bishop, no king!" And James, you will remember, was known as "the wisest fool in Christendom."

(3) Their interest in education. The Roman Catholic Church of the sixteenth century, forbade the reading of the Bible by the people. The Church of England, while it did not forbid it, certainly did not encourage it. But the study of the Bible by laymen was the very corner-stone of Calvinism. It followed, therefore, that Calvinism could not flourish unless the people could read and understand the Scriptures. Hence

John Knox was perfectly logical when he exclaimed, "Let the people be taught!" Education, therefore, became, under that system, the handmaid of religion, for the Presbyterian Church of Scotland thoroughly understood that if it was to stand and grow it must link hands with the school.

These characteristics the Scotch Lowlanders carried with them to Ireland. Ireland, as you know, has always been a thorn in the side of England, and even today the government of Ireland is perhaps the most difficult and serious of England's domestic problems. In the sixteenth and seventeenth centuries the problem was vastly more difficult. Ireland was simply a conquered country whose people, highly excitable, deeply patriotic, and semi-barbarous in civilization, were ever ready upon the slightest pretext to break out into rebellion. The problem was intensified by the fact that their rulers were representatives not only of an alien race but also of a hateful religion. With the Irishman, as with the Scotchman, religion is the prime factor in his life, but between the two there is a vast difference. They represent types as far apart as the poles. Whereas, as I have already pointed out, religion with the Scotchman is the result of intellectual convictions, with the Irishman it is an emotional sentiment. The typical Irishman is perhaps the most emotional being on earth, and in no respects are his sentiments more intense than in his devotion to his Church and his love of country. In fact with the Irishman religion and patriotism are synonymous terms. For century after century he has seen his Church attacked, oppressed, and outlawed by the same powerful enemy which has conquered his country, and as a result he has come to identify the cause of each as the cause of the other.

Thus in her relations with Ireland, for generation after generation, England has assumed an attitude of hostility to the two most powerful national sentiments of the Irish race—patriotism and religion—and for more than three hundred years the history of Ireland has been an almost continuous history of tyranny on the part of her rulers, and rebellion on the part of her people.

Such was the history of Ireland, particularly in the great province of Ulster, in the North, throughout the reign of Queen Elizabeth. So when James VI of Scotland, upon the death of Elizabeth, ascended the throne of England as James I, he found the province of Ulster in a deplorable condition. The English government there was scarcely recognized by the people at all, and was a pure military despotism. The province was divided into ten districts, over each of which was a military commander in civil affairs and a bishop of the Church of England in ecclesiastical matters. It would be difficult to say which of the two was the more hateful to the natives. Ireland, like the Scotch Highlands, was inhabited by clansmen, who obeyed the laws and usages of the clan, and were loyal to their native chieftains. Like the chiefs of the Highlanders these Irish chiefs kept the country in a state of continuous rebellion against the English government. After the suppression of each rebellion, the British government confiscated the lands of the conquered, until finally practically all of the great province of Ulster, embracing six large counties, containing four million acres of land, passed into the hands of the King. Soon after coming to the throne, King James determined on a plan of far-reaching importance with regard to Ulster. This plan was to take possession of the finest portions of this great tract of country, and to transfer the ownership of the land from Irish Catholics to Scotch Presbyterians, thus introducing a Scottish population in place of an Irish one, and Scotch Protestantism in place of Irish Catholicism.

To secure settlers for this purpose, King James naturally looked to that portion of Scotland nearest to Ireland. If you will examine the map of the British Isles you will observe that the Western Lowlands of Scotland, where dwelt the Scotch Presbyterians whom I have described, are separated from the North of Ireland by the North Channel which is there only about twenty miles wide. Here James found the people who, of all his subjects, were best suited to his purpose. They possessed an intense racial pride and, therefore, could be depended upon not to intermarry with the Irish. They were the most intense of Protestants and, therefore, could be depended upon to resist the attacks of Catholicism. They were firm even to obstinacy in character, and as they would owe their lands in Ireland to the generosity of the King they could be depended upon to uphold, support, and maintain his Crown against all opposition. Accordingly in 1609 the lands of Ulster were surveyed, and the next year the settlers began to arrive. During the next ten years from 30,000 to 40,000 Scotch Lowlanders were settled in Ulster. They represented one of the most industrious, law-abiding and intelligent races in Europe. In Ulster, "they drained the swamps, felled the forests, sowed wheat and flax, raised cattle and sheep, began the manufacture of linen and woolen cloth, and not only made their own goods . . . but began the exportation of linen and woolen cloth to

England."[3]   As Greene says: "In its material result
the Plantation of Ulster was undoubtedly a brilliant
success.   Farms and homesteads, churches and mills,
rose fast amid the desolate wilds of Tyrone. . . .
The foundations of the economic prosperity which has
raised Ulster high above the rest of Ireland in wealth
and intelligence were undoubtedly laid in the confisca-
tion of 1610."

The history of the Scotch in Ireland is one of the
most interesting stories in human annals, but I can
dwell on it here only long enough to note the influence
which their residence in Ireland had on their character.   As a minority in the midst of an overwhelming
majority, as aliens surrounded by a bitterly hostile
native population, but two courses were open to the
Scotch in Ireland,—they must either succumb to the
force of the majority, sink their own identity in that
of the natives, and become themselves Irish; or they
must hold themselves absolutely apart from the native
population, and develop more and more the social, religious, and racial differences between the two peoples.
If you have followed the description I have given of
the Scotch character, you will have no doubt as to
which of these alternatives the Scotch in Ireland
adopted.   In the midst of Irish Catholicism their Protestantism became more and more intensely Protestant.
Seeing among the poverty-stricken Irish population
the results of shiftlessness and improvidence in industrial affairs, the Scotch laid yet greater emphasis
upon industry and frugality, and became remarkable
for their comfortable homes and appearances, their

---

3. McKelway: The Scotch-Irish in North Carolina (*Booklet*, IV, 11).

regular conduct and perseverance in business. Surrounded by a population which they regarded as much their inferior, the racial pride of the Scotch, already deep and strong, became yet deeper and stronger, until the Scotchman in Ireland became a more intense Scotchman than the Scotchman in Scotland. In some respects the effects of his residence in Ireland, under the peculiar circumstances which I have described, were anything else but admirable. If it confirmed and strengthened his religious convictions, it tended at the same time to make him a bigot; if it developed industrial and frugal habits, it tended at the same time to develop greed and penuriousness; if it strengthened racial instincts, it tended at the same time to encourage pride and vaingloriousness. "The fact that he was the royal colonist wrought in him the pride, the contempt, the hauteur and swaggering daring of a victorious race planted among a despised race." "The scorn of the Scot was met by the curse of the Celt," and intermarriages between members of the two races were so rare and uncommon as to be anomalous. The Scotch people kept to the Scotch people, so that the Scotch-Irish, as has been so forcibly said, are in reality "Scotch through and through, they are Scottish out and out, and they are Irish because, in the Providence of God, they were sent for some generations" to dwell in the Emerald Isle.

From Ireland descendants of these Scotch settlers came to America. Anomalous as it may seem, it is yet true that the immediate cause of this second emigration arose out of the fact that the Scotch settlement in Ireland had succeeded too well. Planted there by King James in 1610 to develop the country industrially and establish a strong Protestant civilization, a century later the success of their industrial enterprises was exciting the envy of their competitors in England, while the tenacity with which they held to their religion gave offense to the bishops and clergy of the Established Church. In these two sources the one economic, the other religious, originated the emigration to America.

I have already mentioned the fact that the early Scotch settlers in Ulster laid the foundation of the woolen and linen manufactures for which that district has become famous. During the next century these enterprises developed rapidly. Out of the swamps of Ulster arose the cities of Belfast, Londonderry, and other manufacturing cities which became strong competitors of the manufacturing districts of England. At the close of the seventeenth century the industrial conditions in England were exceedingly unprosperous, and the English manufacturers imagined that they were being ruined by the competition of Ireland in the woolen trade. In 1698 accordingly the British Parliament petitioned the King for protection, and at his command the Irish Parliament, which was totally subservient to the King, passed an act forbidding the exporting of woolen goods from that country. This was later followed by a second act forbidding the exportation of such goods to any country except to England. Thus the Irish wool growers and manufacturers were placed absolutely at the mercy of their English rivals who were able to fix their own prices for the Irish products.

About the same time severe penal laws were enacted against the Roman Catholics and all dissenters from the Established Church. The reign of Queen Anne was essentially "a High Church regime" and the High Church party, led by the bishops, ruled supreme in the

Irish Parliament. They could see but little choice between the Roman Catholicism which King James wished to stamp out, and the Presbyterianism which he had used for his purpose. Under their leadership, therefore, the Irish Parliament passed a series of statutes forbidding the exercise of the Roman Catholic religion, and greatly restricting the worship of the Presbyterians. A test act was passed which required all persons who held any office under the government, all persons acting in town councils, and all persons practicing law, to take the communion according to the forms prescribed by the Church of England. This, of course, Presbyterians refused to do, and as practically all such places in Ulster were filled by Presbyterians they were all immediately driven out of their offices. The political persecution was followed by a series of fines and imprisonments for those exercising the Presbyterian form of worship, and by social ostracism. Presbyterian school-masters, guilty of discharging their duties, were liable to imprisonment. The doors of Presbyterian churches were nailed up, and an effort was made in the Irish Parliament to have an act passed declaring marriages performed by Presbyterian clergymen illegal and void. As one historian has expressed it, "All over Ulster there was an outburst of Episcopal tyranny."

Of course no high-spirited, liberty-loving, energetic people would for an instant think of enduring such a situation. Finding reform impossible in Ireland, the Scotch-Irish, as we may now call them, looked to America for relief, and for fifty years before the beginning of the American Revolution left Ireland in crowds, taking with them their families, never to return. In 1718, there is mention of "both ministers and

6

people going off." In 1728 Archbishop Boulter stated
that "above 4,200 men, women and children have been
shipped off from hence for the West Indies within
three years." In 1740, a famine in Ulster "gave an
immense impulse" to emigration, and it was estimated
that during the next several years the annual flow to
America amounted to 12,000 persons. From 1771 to
1773 "the whole emigration from Ulster is estimated
at 30,000, of whom 10,000 were weavers." [4] Of this
emigration, Froude says: "And now commenced the
Protestant emigration, which robbed Ireland of the
bravest defenders of the English interests, and peopled
the American seaboard with fresh flights of Puritans.
Twenty thousand left Ulster on the destruction of the
woolen trade. Many more were driven away by the
first passing of the Test Act. . . . Men of spirit
and energy refused to remain in a country where they
were held as unfit to receive the rights of citizens;
and thenceforward, until the spell of tyranny was
broken in 1782, annual shiploads of families poured
themselves out from Belfast and Londonderry. The
resentment which they carried with them continued
to burn in their new homes; and in the War of Independence, England had no fiercer enemies than the
grandsons and great-grandsons of the Presbyterians
who had held Ulster against Tyrconnell." [5]

Though a few of these settlers landed at Charleston
and moved up the banks of the Pee Dee, the Catawba,
and the Broad rivers, to the hill country of North
Carolina and South Carolina, the great majority of
them landed at Philadelphia. Many of these bought
lands and settled in Pennsylvania, others moved south-

---

4. Hanna: The Scotch-Irish, I, 621-22.
5. The English in Ireland, I, 392.

ward into the western parts of Virginia and North
Carolina. The reason for this is stated by our early
governors to be the high price of lands in Pennsylvania, which, declared Governor Johnston in 1751,
was already "overstocked with people." In 1752
Bishop Spangenberg, the leader of the Moravians in
North Carolina, declared that many settlers came here
from England, Scotland, and the northern colonies,
"on account of poverty, as they wished to own lands
and were too poor to buy in Pennsylvania or New
Jersey." To the same effect wrote Governor Dobbs
in 1755. He declared that as many as ten thousand
immigrants from Holland, Britain, and Ireland had
landed at Philadelphia in a single season, and consequently many were "obliged to remove to the southward for want of lands to take up" in Pennsylvania.
There was still another very important reason for the
large immigration of Scotch-Irish settlers into North
Carolina. During the thirty years from 1734 to 1765
the chief executives of North Carolina were Gabriel
Johnston, who came here from Scotland, and Matthew
Rowan and Arthur Dobbs, who were both Scotch-Irish-
men from Ulster. All three of these governors were
active in their efforts to induce Scotch and Scotch-
Irish immigrants to settle in North Carolina.
"Through these three men, their relatives, friends, con-
nections and acquaintances in the north of Ireland and
the south of Scotland, North Carolina was, perhaps,
better known there than in any other part of the old
world." [6]

The route which these settlers followed from Pennsylvania to North Carolina is plainly laid down on the

---

6. Saunders, W. L.: Prefatory Notes to Colonial Records
of North Carolina, V, xl.

maps of that day. It is called "The Great Road from
the Yadkin River through Virginia to Philadelphia,"
and ran from Philadelphia through Lancaster and
York in Pennsylvania, to Winchester in Virginia, up
the Shenandoah Valley, thence southward across the
Dan River to the Moravian settlements on the Yadkin
River. The distance was 435 miles. On this route
Colonel William L. Saunders, in his Prefatory Notes
to the Colonial Records of North Carolina, makes the
following interesting comment: "Remembering the
route General Lee took when he went into Pennsylvania on that memorable Gettysburg campaign, it will
be seen that very many of the North Carolina boys,
both of German and of Scotch-Irish descent, in following their great leader, visited the homes of their
ancestors and went hither by the very route by which
they came away. To Lancaster and York counties, in
Pennsylvania, North Carolina owes more of her population than to any other known part of the world, and
surely there never was a better population than they
and their descendants—never better citizens, and certainly never better soldiers."[7]

The date of the first Scotch-Irish settlers in North
Carolina is 1735. At a meeting of the Governor's
Council, November 29th of that year, Governor Johnston informed the members that he had received a letter from Arthur Dobbs, "and some other gentlemen of
distinction in Ireland," and Mr. Henry McCulloch, a
merchant of London, "respecting their intention of
sending over to this province several poor Protestant
families with design of raising flax and hemp." They
accordingly asked for a grant of 60,000 acres of land

---

7. Saunders, W. L.: Prefatory Notes to Colonial Records of
   North Carolina.

in New Hanover county on Black River; and their request was granted. The following year the settlers arrived and organized themselves into two congregations, known as Goshen and the Grove. But the tide of Scotch-Irish immigrants which followed a few years later flowed farther to the westward into what are now the counties of Guilford, Orange, Alamance, Caswell, Rowan, Iredell, Cabarrus, Mecklenburg, Lincoln, and Gaston. In 1751 Governor Johnston wrote: "Inhabitants flock in here daily, mostly from Pennsylvania and other parts of America, and some directly from Europe. They commonly seat themselves toward the west and have got near the mountains." Bishop Spangenberg in 1752 declared that "there are many people coming here because they are informed that stock does not require to be fed in the winter season. Numbers of [Scotch-] Irish have therefore moved in, but they will find themselves deceived because if they do not feed their stock in winter they will find to their cost that they will perish." How rapidly these immigrants poured into North Carolina is shown by a letter from Matthew Rowan, acting-governor, in 1753. He writes: "In the year 1746 I was up in the country that is now Anson, Orange, and Rowan counties. There were not then above one hundred fighting men [i. e., a total population of less than 500]; there is now at least three thousand, for the most part Irish Protestants and Germans, and daily increasing." This means that within six years the population of five hundred had grown to at least fifteen thousand. Another indication of the rapid increase of population on the western frontier is the dates of the formation of new counties in that section. You should bear in mind that these counties as they now exist, though still retaining

their old names, have not retained their original
boundary lines: the frontier county, in colonial days,
had no western boundary, but extended as far westward as white population extended. Accordingly
every time a county was formed from the western end
of an existing county, we know that white population
had moved farther westward. In 1746 Edgecombe,
Craven, and Bladen had such far-reaching boundaries.
But so rapidly had population increased in the west
that in that year Granville was cut off from the western
part of Edgecombe, Johnston from Craven, and three
years later, Anson from Bladen. The boundaries of
these counties extended to the mountains and beyond.
In 1752 Orange, still farther westward, was taken
from Granville, Johnston and Bladen, and in 1753
Rowan was cut off from Anson. Nine years later
another part of Anson, still farther to the westward,
was taken to form Mecklenburg, which had become the
center of Scotch-Irish settlements. Thus within sixteen years, as a result of the influx of Scotch-Irish
and German immigrants into Piedmont Carolina, it
was necessary to erect six new counties for their con-
venience.

About the only professions represented among these
early Scotch-Irish settlers were the ministry, teaching,
and surveying, and frequently these three were represented by a single individual. Later, after the settlement became well established, lawyers found their way
thither. Among the settlers the trades were well represented. There were weavers, joiners, coopers, wheel-
wrights, wagon-makers, tailors, blacksmiths, hatters,
merchants, laborers, wine-makers, rope-makers, and
fullers. Practically all were farmers, occupying small
tracts of land, and doing their own work. Accord-

ingly children were regarded as an industrial asset, and large families prevailed. In 1755 Governor Dobbs declared that the Scotch-Irish family usually numbered from five to ten children. But, as Dr. McKelway says, their chief wealth was "in their own capacity to manufacture what they needed. When the goods brought with them began to wear out, the blacksmith built his forge, the weaver set up his loom, and the tailor brought out his goose. A tannery was built on the nearest stream and mills for grinding the wheat and corn were erected on the swift water courses. Saw mills were set up, and logs were turned into plank. The women not only made their own dresses, but the material as well, spinning the wool and afterwards the cotton into lindsey and checks and dyeing it according to the individual taste. . . . In other words, the people were an industrial as well as an industrious people." [8]

It is a rather difficult task to arrive at a just estimate of the character of the Scotch-Irish. There is perhaps no virtue in the whole catalogue of human virtues which has not been ascribed to them; no great principle of human liberty in our political and social system which has not been placed to their credit; no great event in our history which they are not said to have caused. Eulogy has exhausted the English tongue in their praise. Today, however, we are dealing with history, not with eulogy. We know that the Scotch-Irishman was domestic in his habits and loved his home and family; but we know also that he was an unemotional being, seldom giving expression to his affections and accordingly presenting to the world the

---

8. Booklet, IV, No. 11.

appearance of great reserve, coldness, and austerity. He was loyal to his own kith and kin, but stern and unrelenting with his enemies. He was deeply and earnestly religious, but the very depth and earnestness of his convictions tended to make him narrow-minded and bigotted. He was law-abiding so long as the laws were to his liking, but when they ceased to be he disregarded them, quietly if possible, forcibly if necessary. Independent and self-reliant, he was somewhat opinionated and inclined to lord it over any who would submit to his aggressions. He was brave, and he loved the stir of battle. He came of a fighting race; the blood of the old Covenanters, of the Ironsides of Cromwell, flowed in his veins, and the beat of the drum, the music of the fife, the call of the bugle aroused his fighting instincts. His whole history shows that he would fight, he would die, but he could never be subdued. In short, in both his admirable and his unadmirable traits, he possessed just the qualities which were needed on the Carolina frontier in the middle of the eighteenth century; and if you have listened closely to my story of his career in Scotland and in Ireland, you will not be surprised that it was he who conquered the great wilderness of the Piedmont Plateau, drove back the savages, and became, as Mr. Roosevelt has said, "the pioneers of our people in their march westward, the vanguard of the army of fighting settlers, who with axe and rifle won their way from the Alleghanies to the Rio Grande and the Pacific."[9]

When the tide of Revolution rolled upon the back-country, the Scotch-Irish were to a man the staunchest of American patriots. They had from the first strenu-

---

9. Winning of the West, I, 134.

ously opposed the policy of the British Ministry, and
as early as May, 1775, as perhaps some of you have
heard, the Scotch-Irish of Mecklenburg county met at
Charlotte and on the last day of that month formed a
new county government, organized the militia, and
elected county officers, "who shall hold and exercise
their several powers by virtue of this choice and independent of the Crown of Great Britain and former
constitution of this Province." Some estimate of their
contribution to our constitutional history may be
formed when we remember that to them we are indebted for the separation of Church and State in our
government; for the clause requiring the establishment of public schools, and for the most democratic
features of our Constitution, particularly the division
of power into three branches, executive, legislative and
judicial. In the military history of the Revolution
they gave to North Carolina Major-General Robert
Howe, Brigadier-Generals William Lee Davidson,
Griffith Rutherford, James Hogan; Colonels Benjamin
Cleveland, Isaac Shelby, and John Sevier. It was the
Scotch-Irish, under Colonel Francis Locke, who, in
1780, crushed the uprising of the Tories at Ramsauer's
Mill and prepared the way for the overthrow of Cornwallis in North Carolina. It was the Scotch-Irish
under Colonel William R. Davie who so harassed the
British army in its invasion of Western North Carolina that its officers baptized Charlotte, the center
of the Scotch-Irish settlements, as the "Hornets' Nest"
of the Revolution. It was the Scotch-Irish under
Cleveland, Sevier, and Shelby who, on the very crest
of King's Mountain, won the most brilliant victory of
the Revolution. And it was largely a Scotch-Irish
army which under General Greene stopped the tri-

umphant march of Lord Cornwallis at Guilford Court
House, compelled him to abandon North Carolina, and
sent him flying into the arms of Washington at Yorktown.

Time does not permit me to follow the contributions of this race to our history subsequent to the Revolution. In politics, in religion, in commerce, in industry, and in education it has furnished a long line of
leaders, around whose names cluster many of the greatest events in our history. We meet them in legislative
chambers, on the bench, in the chief executive's chair.
More than one-fourth of our governors since the Revolution claimed descent from Scotch-Irish ancestors.
The first president of the University, and the first
Superintendent of Public Instruction, were of this
virile race. In national affairs the Scotch-Irish of
North Carolina have been represented by senators,
congressmen, cabinet officials, and presidents. From
the Scotch-Irish of Mecklenburg county alone sprung
two Presidents of the United States, Andrew Jackson
and James K. Polk, while Andrew Johnson was also
of this race. You see, therefore, that I cannot tell the
story of the Scotch-Irish in North Carolina since the
Revolution, without telling in a large measure, the history of the State, and to do that would require more
time and more patience than you have available.

V

The Germans in North Carolina

In the year 1773, while North Carolina was yet a colony of Great Britain, an English traveler set out on a journey of exploration from Hillsboro across the Blue Ridge Mountains. No well-marked highways directed him unerringly toward his destination, but innumerable trails and winding paths, zigzagging in all directions and crossing each other at a dozen different points, led him hither and thither through the gloomy forests, seemingly beginning nowhere and leading nowhere. Hunters and trappers might have followed them easily enough, but the traveler, having no such keen eyes as theirs, found it difficult to distinguish their faint outlines. The prospect before him, unpromising as it was, was not relieved by the following interesting fact, which he records in his account of his journey. "It was also unlucky for me," he declares, "that the greater number of the inhabitants on the plantations where I called to inquire my way, being Germans, neither understood my questions nor could render themselves intelligible to me." [1]

Let us inquire who were these people here in North Carolina who could neither speak nor understand English, where they came from, and what they came for. Had the English traveler made his journey from Hillsboro a few years earlier he would now and then have met queer processions moving slowly along the

---

1. Smyth, J. F. D.: A Tour in the United States of America, I, 236.

great wilderness road which led southward from Pennsylvania to the Yadkin Valley in North Carolina. First would come a drove of cows, pigs and sheep trotting complaisantly toward him, followed closely by red-faced men and boys in the plain work-a-day clothes of the pioneer farmer. A canvas-covered wagon, stuffed with household goods, feather beds, and farming implements, drawn by a pair or perhaps four stout horses, rumbling over roots and rocks and into holes and gullies, would have brought up the rear. The traveler would have observed that the bed of this wagon was very low, but that it ran up high in the rear, under which feed troughs, pots, kettles, and water buckets dangled outside. From beneath the heavy canvas cover bright-eyed, rosy-cheeked children would have popped out their frowsy white heads to stare at the stranger or at the sights of the new country. From underneath the wagon the dogs, faithful sentinels of the camp, would have growled at the intruder and displayed their long white teeth. Had the stranger stopped this odd procession and asked who these travelers were, whence they came, and whither they were going, he would have received an answer in the same unknown tongue which he heard in 1773.

These patient movers were German immigrants coming into North Carolina from Pennsylvania. Various motives prompted their migrations. Some came in search of adventure and good hunting grounds. Others were looking for good lands. Still others were inspired by religious motives. The first and smallest of these three groups became hunters and trappers, and in the vast unknown forests that extended along the foothills of the Alleghanies and covered the mountain sides, they chased the fox and the deer, hunted the

buffalo and the bear, shot the wolf and the panther,
and trapped the beaver and the otter. With the open-
ing of the spring they would gather up their store of
skins and furs, and turning their backs upon the
wilderness seek the settlements, frequently going as
far northward as Philadelphia, to dispose of their
winter's harvests. Those who came in search of land
of course found it plentiful, cheap, and fertile. The
only capital needed on the Carolina frontier was thrift,
energy, and commonsense, and these characteristics the
Germans possessed in a marked degree. Accordingly
many thousands of them, driven from the Fatherland
by unfavorable conditions, carved handsome estates for
themselves and their children out of the American
wilderness; and at the outbreak of the Revolution the
banks of the Yadkin and the Catawba rivers were
dotted with their neat, pleasant farms and their plain
but comfortable cabins. A third class of Germans
came to Carolina in search of religious freedom and
of fields for missionary activity. Like their neighbors,
the Scotch-Irish, they were moved by a fervent religious zeal. In the unsettled political conditions of
Germany they had frequently been disturbed and sometimes persecuted because of their religious faith, and
those terrible civil wars of that period, waged in the
personal interests of their rulers, often swept away at
a single blow the savings of years. Looking beyond
the Atlantic they beheld a vast continent where men
were free from the burdens of constant civil war, and
where they worshipped God as they pleased. To
America, therefore, despite the discomforts and dangers of an eighteenth century sea voyage, thousands of
them turned as to a haven of refuge and a land of
promise, many of whom, however, were inspired less

by a desire to seek religious freedom for themselves
than by a purpose to carry the gospel to the Indians.
They found their first American homes in Pennsyl-
vania, but from the years 1740 to 1775 a stream
poured into the Piedmont section of North Carolina,
settling in the territory then embraced in Anson and
Granville counties, but now included in the counties of
Orange, Rowan, Guilford, Burke, Lincoln, Randolph,
Iredell, Stokes, Cabarrus, Davidson, Stanly, Catawba,
Alamance, and Forsyth. These immigrants repre-
sented three branches of the Protestant Church—the
Lutheran, the German Reformed, and the Unitas
Fratrum, or Moravian.

The German settlers, though thoroughly law-abiding
and patriotic, took but little interest in politics. The
isolation of their situation on the extreme western
frontier, their ignorance of the English language, and
their lack of political experience made their participa-
tion in the political affairs of the colony extremely
difficult. They were willing to leave the management
of the public business to the English and the Scotch,
to whom politics came as second nature, while they
devoted their energies to their religious, industrial
and social affairs. In another very important respect
the Germans differed from their English fellow-coun-
trymen. The English in North Carolina following a
strong bent toward individualism, settled on large and
widely scattered plantations and developed an agricultural civilization based upon negro slave labor; the
Germans, on the other hand, manifested a decided
tendency toward communism, which led them to settle
in compact communities, with the church and school
as the center, and resulted in the development of an
industrial civilization based on free white labor.

There were several such communities among the German settlements in North Carolina, but the one best adapted to our study is, of course, Wachovia. This is true not only because the development of the Wachovia settlement as an industrial community has been more complete than any other, but also because its records from the beginning of the settlement to the present day have been perfectly preserved and afford an opportunity for an historical study not found in any other community in North Carolina. To Wachovia as a typical German community in North Carolina I shall, accordingly, direct your attention.

The history of Wachovia begins in the year 1752. In that year a company of Moravians, moved by a desire to find a home free from religious persecution, by a purpose to preach the gospel to the Indians, and by a wish to develop a community on their own peculiar principles without let or hindrance from outside influences, determined to plant a settlement in North Carolina. With that thoroughness which is one of the most marked characteristics of the German people, they sent out an exploring party under the leadership of Bishop Augustus Gottlieb Spangenberg, to view the land and select the site for the colony. Spangenberg's party set out on their tour from Edenton and crossed the entire length of North Carolina to the very summit of the Blue Ridge Mountains where they viewed the headwaters of streams that rise in North Carolina and flow into the Mississippi River. A diary[2] in which the good Bishop recorded the minutest details of their expedition tells us in simple and impressive lan-

---

2. An English translation is printed in Colonial Records of North Carolina, V, 1-14.

guage the story of the dangers and hardships which they encountered. Sickness, cold, and hunger were among the least of their sufferings. After a thorough and painstaking survey, the party selected a tract of land in what is now Forsyth county containing about 100,000 acres. "As regards this land," wrote the Bishop, "I regard it as a corner which the Lord has reserved for the Brethren. . . . The situation of this land is quite peculiar. It has countless springs and many creeks; so that as many mills can be built as may be desirable. These streams make many and fine meadow lands. . . . The stock would have excellent pasturage and might be kept for a number of winters among the reeds on the creeks. . . . The most of this land is level and plain; the air fresh and healthy, and the water is good, especially the springs, which are said not to fail in summer. . . . In the beginning a good forester and hunter will be indispensable. The wolves and bears must be extirpated as soon as possible, or stock raising will be pursued under difficulties. The game in this region may also be very useful to the Brethren in the first years of the colony." Thus we see that the Bishop was impressed with the advantages which the country offered for the development of just such an industrial community as Wachovia afterwards became.

It was Bishop Spangenberg who called the settlement Wachovia. The word is derived from two German words, "wach," a meadow, and "aue," a stream. Wachovia lay within the possessions of Lord Granville and from him the Moravian Brethren purchased it in August 1753. Two months later their plans were completed, and October 8, 1753, twelve unmarried men set out from the Moravian settlement at Bethlehem, Pennsylvania, to break ground for the settlement of Wachovia in North Carolina. No better evidence is needed of the shrewd, commonsense of these German settlers than the simple fact that this small band, whose mission was to lay the foundation of civilization in the wilderness, consisted of a minister of the gospel, a warden, a physician, a tailor, a baker, a shoemaker and tanner, a gardener, three farmers, and two carpenters. In the industrial community which they went out to found there was to be no place for drones. It is also interesting to note that they were fully conscious of the significance of their undertaking. Looking far into the future with rare vision they foresaw the growth and development of their community and the intense interest with which posterity would inquire into its beginnings. Accordingly from the very first they recorded their daily doings to the minutest and most trivial details. There is but one other instance in our history of such foresight, *i. e.* the colony which Baron de Graffenreid planted at the confluence of the Neuse and Trent rivers, and of which he himself left for posterity a most interesting account.

The little band of Moravian Brethren made their journey from Pennsylvania to Carolina in a large covered wagon drawn by six horses. Their route carried them over mountains wild and rugged, into forests dense and dark, and across rivers whose banks were so steep that frequently the travelers had to grade them before their wagon could enter the streams. Nearly six weeks were required for the trip. When they left Pennsylvania they were oppressed with heat; when they reached North Carolina the ground was covered with snow. At 3 o'clock Saturday afternoon, November 17, they reached the spot where now stands the

7

town of Bethabara, better known in its immediate neighborhood as "Old Town." There they found shelter in a log cabin which had been built but afterwards abandoned by a German adventurer named Hans Wagoner. It was an humble abode, without a floor and with a roof full of cracks and holes, but in it the Brethren held their first divine service and had their first love feast. Sunday was observed as a day of real rest, but was followed by weeks of earnest, manly toil. One of their first cares was to enlarge their cabin and to lay in a supply of provisions for the winter. Their rifles supplied them with game in abundance. Salt was procured from Virginia, flour and corn from the Scotch-Irish settlements on the Yadkin, and beef from those on the Dan. In December they sowed their first wheat. A few days later came the Christmas season, and on Christmas Eve they gathered around the great open fire in their log cabin to hear again the wonderful story of Bethlehem. "We had a little love feast," says their faithful journal; "then near the Christ Child we had our first Christmas Eve in North Carolina, and rested in peace in this hope and faith. . . . All this while the volves and panthers howled and screamed in the forests near by."

Throughout their first year the Moravian Brethren kept steadily at their tasks, and before the year had gone they had in operation a carpenter shop, a tailoring establishment, a pottery, a blacksmith shop, a shoe shop, a tannery and a cooper shop; had harvested wheat, corn, tobacco, flax, millet, barley, oats, buckwheat, turnips, cotton, garden vegetables; had cleared and cultivated fields, cut roads through the forests, built a mill and erected several cabins. They made long journeys, going as far north as Philadelphia and as far south as Wilmington. The physician, Dr. Lash, made trips twenty, fifty and even a hundred miles through the forests to visit the sick and relieve the suffering. The Brethren had many visitors who came long distances to consult the physician or to secure the services of the shoemaker or the tailor. There was but little money in the backwoods, and sometimes these visitors paid for the purchases in ways that were odd and amusing. A stranger passing through Wachovia wanted to buy a pair of shoes, but having no money, he agreed in payment for them to cut down and trim one hundred trees! Within three months, during the year 1754, 103 visitors came to Wachovia. The next year the number was 426. Visitors became so numerous that the Brethren decided to build a "strangers' house." This was the second building in Wachovia. Four days after it was finished it was occupied by a man and his invalid wife who came to consult the physician. Travel between Wachovia and Pennsylvania was frequent and the little colony continued to grow. More unmarried men and later a few married couples came from Pennsylvania, and by 1756 the Bethabara colony numbered sixty-five souls. Until the outbreak of the French and Indian War, the Moravians were on friendly terms with the Indians. Indeed, one of their purposes in coming to North Carolina was to preach the gospel to them. They treated the Indians kindly, and the Indians spoke of the fort at Bethabara as "the Dutch fort, where there are good people and much bread." But with the breaking out of the war the savages became hostile, and their enmity gave the Moravian Brethren much trouble. The Brethren were compelled to build a fort, to arm every man in the colony, and to place sentinels around the settlement. Many

thrilling incidents occurred during the war, and the
Moravians were frequently called on to render services
to their white neighbors. From thirty and forty miles
around families sought refuge at Bethabara where all
learned to love and respect the Moravian Brethren,
some even applying for membership in the Moravian
Church.

After the close of the war the settlement grew more
rapidly. Two towns, Bethabara and Bethania, were
founded before 1760, but from the first the Brethren
intended that the chief town should be in the center of
Wachovia, and they thought the closing of the Indian
War and the reestablishment of peace a favorable time
to begin it.

The first act in the founding of this new town, which
received the name of Salem, took place January 6,
1766. During the singing of a hymn the work was begun by clearing a site for the first house, and on February 19th eight young men moved into it. Other
houses were then erected in quick succession, and during the next year many of the Bethabara community
moved to Salem, where they were joined by more
Brethren from Bethlehem, and even by a goodly number directly from Germany. Salem soon became the
principal settlement of the Moravians in North Carolina. The same man whose adventure in the Carolina
wilderness I described in the beginning of this lecture,
visited Salem in 1773 and left an interesting description of the town and its people as it appeared just upon
the eve of the Revolution. Leaving Salisbury he went
first to Bethania and then to Bethabara. "This town,"
he said, "is ten miles from the other; but being informed that Salem was the principal, I immediately
proceeded on after breakfast, and arrived there about

noon. . . . This society, sect, or fraternity of The
Moravians have everything in common, and are possessed of a very large and extensive property. . . .
From their infancy they are instructed in every branch
of useful and common literature, as well as in mechani-
cal knowledge and labour. . . . The Moravians
have many excellent and very valuable farms, on which
they make large quantities of butter, flour, and provisions, for exportation. They also possess a number of
useful and lucrative manufactures, particularly a very
extensive one of earthen ware, which they have
brought to great perfection, and supply the whole country with it for some hundred miles around. In short,
. . . they certainly are valuable subjects, and by
their unremitting industry and labor have brought a
large extent of wild, rugged country into a high state
of population and improvement."[3]

Thirteen years later, just at the close of the Revolution, another traveler visited Wachovia, and left us
his impression of the Moravian settlement.[4] After
visiting the Guilford Battle Ground, he says:

"I pursued the route of Cornwallis in his advance,
and entered the possessions of the happy Moravians, so
justly distinguished for their piety, industry, and admirable police. The road from Guilford to Salem was
good, and the country pleasant. . . . In the general face of the country. . . . this region closely
resembles the South of France. . . .

"The moment I touched the boundary of the Moravians, I noticed a marked and most favorable change in

---

3. Smyth: Vol. 1, Chapter XXIX.
4. Watson, Elkanah: Men and Times of the Revolution,
   292-94.

the appearance of buildings and farms; and even the cattle seemed larger, and in better condition. Here, in combined and well-directed effort, all put shoulders to the wheel, which apparently moves on oily springs. We passed, in our ride, New Garden, a settlement of Quakers from Nantucket. They too, were exemplary and industrious. The generality of the planters in this State depend upon negro labor, and live scantily in a region of affluence. In the possessions of the Moravians and Quakers, all labor is performed by whites. Every farm looks neat and cheerful; the dwellings are tidy and well furnished, abounding in plenty.

"In the evening, I attended service at the Moravian chapel. This was a spacious room in a large edifice, adorned with that neat and simple elegance, which was a peculiar trait of these brethren and their Quaker neighbors. On our first entrance, only two or three persons were visible; but, the moment the organ sounded, several doors were simultaneously opened. The men were ushered in on one side, and the women on the other; and in one minute the seats were filled, and the devotees arranged for worship. The devotions, on that occasion, were merely chanting a melodious German anthem, accompanied by an organ.

"In the morning, I was introduced to Mr. Bargee, their principal. He conducted me through all their manufactories, and communicated to me, with much intelligence, many facts in relation to the tenets and habits of this devout and laborious sect. Salem comprehended about forty dwellings, and occupies a pleasant situation. . . . Every house in Salem was supplied with water, brought in conduits a mile and a half."

In 1791 the Moravian Brethren had the honor of
entertaining at Salem George Washington, President
of the United States. In taking his leave after a
round of festivities, Washington addressed a letter to
"The United Brethren of Wachovia" in which he said:
"From a society whose governing principles are industry and love of order much may be expected toward
the improvement and prosperity of the country in
which their settlements are formed, and experience
authorizes the belief that such will be obtained." Washington's words were prophetic. The influence of the
Moravian Brethren, although exerted so unostenta-
tiously as to pass almost unnoticed, has been altogether
out of proportion to their numerical strength. The
thousands of visitors who have been attracted to
Wachovia by the peculiarity of their customs have returned to their homes profoundly impressed by the sincerity of their religious devotions, their zeal for education, and their remarkable skill in the development
of large industrial enterprises. It is surely no acci-
dent that the oldest college for young women in the
Southern States is located in their midst; nor was it
a freak of chance that the most important manufacturing city in North Carolina should be the twin sister of
Salem.

These customs and characteristics of the German
settlers were, perhaps, more accentuated in Wachovia
than anywhere else in North Carolina, but they were
by no means confined to the Moravians. Had we paid
a visit, let us say one hundred years ago, to Lincolnton,
Salisbury, Concord, and their neighboring communities, we should have found that Salem was but a well-
developed type of the several German communities in
the State. Everywhere the people would have greeted

us in the German language, or a corrupted form of it
known as "Pennsylvania Deutsch." At this time, too,
the names of the people retained not only their German
pronunciation, but also their German spelling. Our
modern Coon was then Kuhn, Barringer was Behrin-
ger, Smith was Schmidt, Williams was Wilhelm. Thus
it happens that many persons in our history whose
names would indicate an English ancestry were really
of German descent.

The houses of the German settlers, usually construct-
ed of logs, were far less pretentious than the manor
houses on the broad plantations of their English countrymen in the East; but they had in a much more
marked degree the charm of simplicity and orderli-
ness; and their farms though smaller were better cultivated, their cattle fatter and sleeker. The superiority
of the German farmer in these respects over the English planter was due not only to his greater industry
and thrift, but also to the difference in his system of
labor. It was the difference between the skilled, care-
ful and energetic labor of the free white man working
under the impetus of self-interest, and the inefficient,
wasteful, compulsory labor of the enslaved negro working under the impulse of the lash. In the German
household everybody worked, including father. They
not only raised their own food, but also made their
own clothes. The women were expert weavers, and
knew how to dye and combine colors into beautiful fab-
rics. Their markets were Cross Creek [Fayetteville],
Columbia and Charleston, and a trip to market was a
very serious and sometimes a dangerous undertaking.
It took four or five weeks to carry a wagonload of
produce to Charleston and bring back supplies for the
farm. Such trips were not made often, and as a con-

sequence the German settlers learned to depend on their own industry and skill for most of their necessities.

The center of the German settlement was the church and the schoolhouse. Generally the same buildings served for both, and the same man as minister and teacher. Their churches at first were built of logs, but as they increased in prosperity these log churches were replaced with frame buildings and sometimes with brick and even stone structures. The principal book in the German home was the Bible. Among the Germans as among the Scotch-Irish the leader of the people was usually the minister. He had need to be not only a scholar, but a man of great physical power and endurance for his office was no sinecure. The people of his congregations were scattered over a large territory, sometimes forty and fifty miles from their churches, and the minister was compelled to take long and lonely rides to visit them. These rides were no child's play. They led him over rough roads, running through dark forests, crossing rivers and creeks without bridges, and took him out in snow as well as in sunshine. He often met danger, too, from wild beasts, for there were still plenty of panthers and wild cats in the woods, and bears frequently crossed his path.

One of these ministers, who came directly from Germany, has left us an interesting account of his work among the German settlers. Landing at Charleston he rode three hundred miles on horseback to Lincolnton. He was fourteen days on the journey, sometimes spending the nights at the homes of settlers and sometimes camping in the woods. But when he reached Lincolnton, he says, the warm welcome he received paid him for all the troubles and discomforts of his

long trip. The people came many miles tó welcome
him. He found them open and frank in their manner
and speech. They knew nothing of compliments, and
did not know how to flatter, but they spoke in a way
that showed they knew how to think. So many of
them invited him to go to their homes that he hardly
knew how to choose. "They helped us to buy a fine
plantation of 200 acres," he said, "and as soon as we
were settled the people from all parts of the country
brought us flour, corn, hams, sausages, dried fruit,
chickens, turkeys, geese, butter, cheese and other things
in such quantities that for many weeks we had no
necessity for spending one penny for housekeeping."

We learn from his story many of the interesting social customs of the German settlers. One incident that
he relates shows their law-abiding character. "One
day," he said, "I passed the courthouse in Lincolnton
at the moment when a man was standing in the pillory.
A German settler called to me to stop a while and see
how Americans punish rogues and thieves. I asked
him: 'This criminal certainly is not a German?' He
replied: 'Never has a German stood in pillory in Lincolnton, nor has a German been hung in this place."

Another characteristic of the Germans was their
humor. They believed thoroughly in the philosophy of
the old rhyme so frequently on their lips,

> "A little nonsense now and then
> Is relished by the best of men."

While at work they worked earnestly, but when holi-
days came they indulged to the fullest degree in their
fun and sports. They loved their Easter celebrations
and their Kris Kringle frolics. Then, too, they had
their quilting parties, their spinning matches, corn

shuckings, log rollings, house raisings, and other amusements that not only afforded fun and frolic for the young, but combined utility with sport. Boxing, wrestling, racing, swimming, and other outdoor sports were favorite pastimes.

In the development of their religious and social life the German settlers had one very decided advantage over the other early settlers in North Carolina. As I have already pointed out they came to the colony in congregations, and settled as communities. This fact of course enabled them to organize churches and schools much more readily than those who settled on widely scattered plantations. Those pioneer schools were exceedingly crude institutions. The schoolhouses were of logs; the cracks were stopped up with red clay; they had no floor except mother earth; the desks were logs trimmed flat on the upper side, with no backs and no rests for the books or the arms. There were no blackboards, maps or pictures. About the only decoration of which such a school could boast was the long hickory rod over the teacher's chair, which, like the sceptre of the king,

> "shows the force of temporal power,
> The attribute to awe and majesty,
> Wherein doth sit the dread and fear of...."

the pedagogue.

Of course, as the settlements grew and prospered, those first schoolhouses gave way to better ones. But even the best were unattractive enough. Pennsylvania and Germany supplied the teachers, many of whom were men of ability and profound scholarship. As a rule they combined the two offices of teacher and preacher in the same person. The text-books used in the schools for many years were all written in the German language, and English was not used at all. It was not until some years after the Revolution that English found its way into these German schools, and even then it had to take a secondary place. The first English school was opened in 1798 in Cabarrus county by John Yeoman. This reform won its way slowly against the opposition of the older settlers who clung tenaciously to the language of their cradles. But their children finding themselves in a State in which all social, commercial and legal transactions were carried on in the English tongue, naturally and properly were unwilling to go through life under the handicap of being ignorant of the very language in which they must transact all of their affairs. Of course English won the day and in time not only ousted the German from the schools, but took its place in the daily affairs of the Germans themselves until their very surnames, as I have said, became Anglicized.

Many of these German schools have interesting histories, a typical one being the Pleasant Retreat Academy of Lincolnton, founded in 1813. "The older students delighted to speak of its refreshing shades—the oak and hickory, interspersed with chestnuts and chinquepins—and the spring at the foot of the hill." Many distinguished men were numbered among its trustees, and its teachers, we are told, were men of ability. But a school, like a tree, is to be judged by its fruits. What kind of students does it have, and what does it do for them? Some of the students of Pleasant Retreat Academy wrote their names high in our annals.

How largely the Germans have influenced, and still influence the educational thought of North Carolina you may infer from the fact that Sidney M. Finger, for eight years state superintendent of public instruction, was of this race; that the president of Salem College and of the State Normal and Industrial College, are both of German descent; and that the superintendents of public schools in at least seven of our counties at this time are men of German ancestry.

It is certainly not without significance that the same year, 1813, which saw the founding of Pleasant Retreat Academy, also saw the erection at Lincolnton of the first cotton mill in North Carolina. The mill, the work of a German, Michael Schenck, was the forerunner of that remarkable industrial development which has placed North Carolina second among the States of the American Union in the manufacture of cotton. How largely this State is indebted to her German population for her industrial development will be readily seen by pointing out the geographical center of the manufacturing industries of North Carolina, and by studying the names of the men behind these enterprises. In 1910 the sixteen counties which I mentioned as having been settled largely by Germans, contained 162 of the 402 cotton, woolen, silk and knitting mills then in the State, or more than 40 per cent. That this industrial development is due primarily to the Germans is shown not only by the names of the pioneers in manufacturing industries in this State— the Schencks, the Frieses, the Holts, the Reinhardts, the Hokes, and many others—but also by an examination of the officials in those manufacturing corporations even of today. These manufacturing enterprises are largely owned or controlled by men of German descent. This industrial development, indeed, is the most striking and important of the contributions of the Germans to our civilization.

But in many other spheres of activity the Germans have contributed leaders,—in war, in politics, in law, in literature, and in religion. To war they gave General Stephen D. Ramseur and General Robert F. Hoke; to politics, Thomas L. Clingman and F. M. Simmons, United States senators; to law, Charles Price, David Schenck, and William A. Hoke; to literature, John H. Boner and Frances Fisher Tiernan, better known to her readers as Christian Reid. In the religious life of the State the Germans have played a part all out of proportion to their numerical strength. Of course in the Lutheran, the German Reformed, and the Moravian Churches the leaders are almost entirely, if not entirely, German. But that their influence is not limited to these religious organizations was strikingly pointed out to me a few days ago, when my attention was called to the fact that at the last session of the Western Conference of the Methodist Episcopal Church, the names of five out of eleven presiding elders chosen, and of sixty-seven, or 29 per cent of the pastors assigned to congregations, indicated that they were of German ancestry.

Throughout our history, the Germans have been the most conservative force in the life of the State. In every crisis they have acted as a steadying influence upon their more volatile countrymen, and when the Englishman, at some fancied trespass upon his property rights, or the Highlander, at some imaginary affront to his personal dignity, or the Scotch-Irishman, at some supposed attack upon his political or religious liberty, has been ready to fly into a passion and upset the whole plan of creation rather than submit to wrong, real or imaginary, the German has moved conservatively, advised caution and patience, and always

stood for the established order and for peace. Thus in
1776 he held back when his English and Scotch countrymen were ready to plunge the country into rebellion
and revolution; in 1860 he opposed slavery and secession. Though he could not prevent revolution in
1776, nor secession in 1860, his influence undoubtedly
went far toward making both those movements more
orderly and less noisy in North Carolina than in some
of her sister states; and so today, he continues to exercise a similar conservative, silent, and unostentatious,
but a most potent and salutary influence, which will
not, indeed, prevent our people from joining in the
progressive tendencies and movements of the age, but
will influence them to do so with cautious thoughtful-
ness and quiet dignity. It is worth much to North
Carolina—much more than will ever be generally real-
ized—that she has in her population the thoughtful,
steadying, conservative influence which is so distinc-
tive of her German citizenship.

BIBLIOGRAPHY

SOURCES:

Clark, Walter (ed.): State Records of North Carolina. Vols. XI-XXVI. 1895-1906. (Continuation of Saunders: Colonial Records.)

Grimes, J. Bryan: Abstracts of North Carolina Wills. 1910.

Grimes, J. Bryan: North Carolina Wills and Inventories. 1912.

Salley, Alexander S., Jr.: Narratives of Early Carolina, 1650-1708. (*Original Narratives of Early American History, J. F. Jameson, Editor.*) 1911.

Saunders, William L. (ed.): The Colonial Records of North Carolina, Vols. I-X. 1886-1890.

AUTOBIOGRAPHIES, TRAVELS, AND MEMOIRS:

Brickell, John: The Natural History of North Carolina. 1737. (J. Bryan Grimes, ed., 1910.)

Catesby, Mark: Natural History of Carolina, Florida, and the Bahama Islands. 1731.

Smyth, J. F. D.: A Tour of the United States of America, 1784.

Watson, Elkanah: Men and Times of the Revolution. 1856.

BIOGRAPHIES:

Alderman, E. A.: William Hooper.

Ashe, Samuel A'Court (ed.): Biographical History of North Carolina from Colonial Times to the Present. 1905-1917.

Caruthers, E. W.: Life and Character of Rev. David Caldwell. 1842.

MacLean, J. P.: Flora MacDonald in America. 1909.

COUNTY AND LOCAL HISTORY:

Arthur, John Preston: Western North Carolina: A History from 1730 to 1913. 1914.

Nash, Francis: Hillsboro, Colonial and Revolutionary. 1903.

Rumple, Jethro: A History of Rowan County. 1881. (Reprinted 1916.)

Tompkins, D. A.: History of Mecklenburg County. 1903.

Brinson, S. M.: The Early History of Craven County. (*North Carolina Booklet*, X-4.)

McNeely, Robert Ney: Union County and the Old Waxhaw Settlement. (*North Carolina Booklet*, XII-1.)

Nash, Francis: The History of Orange County. (*North Carolina Booklet*, IX-3.)

GENERAL HISTORIES:

Ashe, Samuel A'Court: History of North Carolina, Vol. I, 1908.

Bancroft, George: History of the United States.

Connor, R. D. W.: History of North Carolina, 1584-1783. 1919.

Wheeler, John H.: Historical Sketches of North Carolina from 1584 to 1851. 1851.

HISTORIES OF SPECIAL TOPICS AND PERIODS:

Bassett, John S.: Landholding in Colonial North Carolina. (*Trinity College Historical Papers, Series II.*) 1898.

Bernheim, G. D., and Cox, George A.: History of the Evangelical Lutheran Synod and Ministerium of North Carolina. 1902.

Cheshire, Joseph B.: How Our Church Came to North Carolina. (*The Spirit of Missions*, LXXXIII-5.)

Clewell, John Henry: History of Wachovia in North Carolina. 1902.

Draper, Lyman C.: King's Mountain and Its Heroes. 1881.

Faust, Albert Bernhardt: The German Element in the United States. 1909.

Fiske, John: Old Virginia and Her Neighbours. 1897.

Foote, William Henry: Sketches of North Carolina: Historical and Biographical. 1846.

Hanna, Charles A.: The Scotch-Irish. 1902.

Historic Sketch of the Reformed Church in North Carolina. 1907.

Knight, Edgar W.: Public School Education in North
Carolina. 1916.

MacLean, J. P.: Scotch-Highlanders in America. 1900.

Nixon, Joseph R.: German Settlers in Lincoln County
and Western North Carolina. (*James Sprunt Historical Publications*, II-2.)

Roosevelt, Theodore: The Winning of the West. 1903.

Smith, Charles Lee: The History of Education in North
Carolina. 1888.

North Carolina Booklet: MacRae, James C.: *The High-
land-Scotch Settlement in North Carolina* (IV-10);
McKelway, A. J.: *The Scotch-Irish of North Carolina*
(IV-11); Graham, William A.: *Battle of Ramsaur's
Mill* (IV-2); Raper, Charles Lee: *Social Life in Co-
lonial North Carolina* (III-5); Pittman, Thomas M.:
Industrial Life in Colonial Carolina (VII-1); Hollo-
day, Alexander Q.: *Social Conditions in Colonial
North Carolina* (III-10); Grimes, J. Bryan: *Some
Notes on Colonial North Carolina, 1700-1750* (V-2);
Smith, Charles Lee: *Schools in Colonial Times*
(VII-4); Haywood, Marshall DeLancey: *The Story of
Queen's College, or Liberty Hall in the Province of
North Carolina* (XI-3).

North Carolina Day Program: (Scotch-Highlanders,
1905); (Scotch-Irish, 1907); (Germans, 1908).